Poetry Ireland REVIEW 96

Eagarthóir / Editor

CAITRÍONA O'REILLY

© Poetry Ireland Ltd 2008

Poetry Ireland Ltd/Éigse Éireann Teo gratefully acknowledges the
assistance of The Arts Council/An Chomhairle Ealaíon and the Arts
Council of Northern Ireland.

Poetry Ireland invites individuals and commercial organisations to become
Friends of Poetry Ireland. For more details please contact:

Poetry Ireland Friends Scheme
Poetry Ireland
2 Proud's Lane
off St Stephen's Green
Dublin 2
Ireland

or telephone +353 1 4789974; e-mail management@poetryireland.ie

PATRONS:
Joan and Joe McBreen   ColourBooks Ltd

ISBN: 1-902121-34-1
ISSN: 0332-2998

ASSISTANT EDITOR: Paul Lenehan, with the assistance of Lucile Dumont & David Maybury

DESIGN: Alastair Keady (**www.hexhibit.com**)
Printed in Ireland by **ColourBooks Ltd** Baldoyle Industrial Estate Dublin 13

Contents

Poetry Ireland Review 96

Molly Bashaw	5	ACHILLES
	6	THE ONION FARMERS
	7	EXPATRIOTISM
Knute Skinner	8	PRETENDING
	10	RINGING THE NUMBER
	11	THE RUINS
Miriam Gamble	12	THE FLAYING OF MARSYAS
	13	SHHHH...
Gina Ferrara	14	WHEN YOU ARRIVE
Aidan Rooney	15	THE WHISPERING GALLERY AT GRAND CENTRAL
Howard Wright	16	SOUTH CITY
	18	SCRAP
Susie DeCoste	19	AFTER ATTEMPTING SUICIDE, AFTER A WEEKEND SNEAK-OUT TO HUNT RABBIT ALONE
Daniel Hardisty	20	MERMAID ALIVE
	21	ELEGY
Enda Coyle-Greene	22	GRACE
Nicholas Bradley	24	LETTER TO THEO
Sam Gardiner	25	DEVIL'S COACH-HORSE
	26	THE CANDLEBLOWER'S RECITER
	28	FEET (A CORONET)
	30	HANDS (A CORONET)
Christina Park	31	DOG LOVE
Mark Roper	32	ESSAY: HALCYON
Darrell Epp	36	THE RIVER
	37	KISSING PIRANHAS
Carrie Etter	38	HOMECOMING
Fergus Allen	40	THE NEW KING OF THE CASTLE
Justin Quinn	42	MUSÍLKOVA
	44	ON THE TRANSLATOR'S ART
	46	COUPLE
John F Deane	48	SNOW FALLING ON CHESTNUT HILL
Gerard Smyth	52	ESSAY: JAMES LIDDY
James Liddy	54	'I DREAMT I DWELT IN MARBLE HALLS'
	55	IN SOUTH BEND
	56	A NEARY'S AFTERNOON
	57	VERSES FOR THE BELMULLET FESTIVAL
Richard Murphy	58	ESSAY: TEA WITH OLIVER ST JOHN GOGARTY
Thomas Kilroy	62	ESSAY: REMEMBERING AUSTIN CLARKE
Conor O'Callaghan	66	THIS FAR SOUTH
	68	AMONG OTHER THINGS
Jesse P Ferguson	69	PILLOW TALK
David Kennedy	70	CÉZANNE AT LES TROIS SAUTETS

Kit Fryatt 72 REVIEW : EILÉAN NÍ CHUILLEANÁIN

Paddy Bushe 76 REVIEW: NUALA NÍ DHOMHNAILL AND VONA GROARKE

Tom Hubbard 83 REVIEW: ENDA COYLE-GREENE, FRED JOHNSTON
AND MARK ROPER

Nessa O'Mahony 86 REVIEW : CATHERINE PHIL MAC CARTHY, JOAN AND
KATE NEWMANN, NUALA NÍ CHONCHÚIR

David Cooke 90 REVIEW : COLETTE BRYCE

Liam Carson 94 REVIEW : ELAINE FEINSTEIN AND MARINA TSVETAEVA

Philip Coleman 99 REVIEW : SEÁN LYSAGHT AND JOHN MCAULIFFE

Notes on Contributors 107

Molly Bashaw

ACHILLES

Your mother sleeps in America
while you cycle over the Swabian Alb, a shadow of hawk,
a shadow of wren on the road.
She has dipped you in the river of her dream.
And what will you call this weakness?

You love the sight of the Ferris wheel, the scream
of skyline, ankles and elbows
raised to the angles of gods.

You love the net of quiet summer lightning, the dogs
who chase you and bite you
on the places your mother held you with her hands.

There is no Germany, no America, you tell yourself, no distance
but the moment of wheels, a clown's whisper
in the nostril of a circus pony.
You shift the stones, lifting off,
like a bird you pull in the soft bones of your feet.

Molly Bashaw

THE ONION FARMERS

Today on the onion field a whale
pulls the oxen cart, takes onions through her baleen.
Her black flukes splash the black sky, the silo,
and she blows onions through her blowhole,
singing high pitched of onionskin.

Even at this we do not stay surprised.
We feel our way to the field again, again
wake the whale with our hands.
We pull onions and onions, roll
them over our hardened, dirty bodies, still looking
for the one that is the sun, for the coin that will save us.

Molly Bashaw

EXPATRIOTISM

America, I have pressed your dahlia,
your corn kernel in glass.
I collect your stamps.

I have eaten your words
(dahlia, corn kernel), swallowed
your stamps. America, I will send you

with stamps to heaven.
They will ask you there, what you believe.
Say, in the dahlia, the corn kernel.

Knute Skinner

PRETENDING

She pretended to be asleep, but that was okay.
That night I was willing enough
to pretend she wasn't pretending.

So I watched her a moment as she lay
with her back turned toward me,
trying to dole out slow, steady exhalations
and trying not to move as I blew soft air
on the back of her neck.

Then after a while I yawned out loud
and got out of bed,
kicking my shoe as I did so
and pretending to stumble.

Then I crossed to the window as if to look out,
not seeing a thing in the dark but just standing there
opening and closing the curtains.

Then I crossed to my dresser where I opened drawers
and then closed them again
and then slid my keys and coins
back and forth on the surface.

Through it all she lay there as still
as if she were dead,
and I spent a few minutes thinking about
what she might be thinking.
Then I walked back toward the bed,
one heavy step at a time,
and looked down at her.

One shoulder, clad in the soft light blue
of her new nightie,
was exposed where I'd pulled back the covers
as I got out of bed.
Perhaps she was feeling a chill.

I studied her shoulder and then moved
to her dressing table.
I took out the stoppers and sniffed her perfumes.
I dabbed her lotions on my neck and rubbed creams
all over my hands.
I opened her box of earrings and snapped it shut.

'Oh, I'm sorry,' I said as she asked me
what I was doing,
'I'm afraid I've woken you up.'

Knute Skinner

RINGING THE NUMBER

Ringing the number,
I let my finger hang in the air.

I think of the one at the other end
of the call I have not yet made.

She is stabbing a cigarette out
and pouring a second or a third cup of tea.

She is slipping out of her faded Chinese robe
and easing a thick leg into sudsy water.

She is painting her nails,
toe after toe in dark scarlet fury.

She is taking her pills, or else
she's neglecting to take them.

And I? I am telling myself
to ring her number.

First published in *The Stony Thursday Book*, No 7, Autumn 2008,
edited by Thomas McCarthy.

Knute Skinner

THE RUINS

Two arms slipped around my waist
as I stood there looking at the ruins.
I'd come a long way to see them.

I'd come thousands of miles to see them,
and I wouldn't have felt let down
no matter how long I stood there looking,
taking in the graceful sweep of broken walls,
the warm greys of fallen stones,
the odd presence of a living past.

I had left her, after our quarrel,
at a small table outside a village café
two or three miles from our modest hotel.
I had set off alone, camera in hand.
It was, after all, what I had come for.

I stood there a long few minutes, rooted,
her arms around me,
breathing hard with unasked-for stress,
confused by the unexpected mix
of vision and touch.
And then I eased her around beside me,
and together, with careful steps,
we passed into the ruins.

I did get a few murky shots
taken later in the gathering dusk,
and I promised myself I'd return the following day.
The next three days, however, came windblown and wet,
and we sat in the forced cheer of the hotel bar.
The day after that the proprietor's talky son
drove us down through the long narrow pass
to our scheduled flight.

Miriam Gamble

THE FLAYING OF MARSYAS

It's said the Muses judged the contest –
that they were pleased by Apollo's superior craft.
His ability to lift the pelt in a single stroke
was greatly lauded. 'See how beautiful the work,
clean as the average man would skin an orange!'
they remarked among themselves. 'Not even a wound
disturbs his fearful symmetry.' Meanwhile Marsyas

lay on, his life force startlingly undiminished,
limbs gesturing in disbelieving contract
with the world. 'This for a stupid pipe,' he roared,
for Marsyas, Ovid relates, possessed the gift
of consciousness: 'for this they cleave me from myself!'
But nobody beyond the forest heard his cries,
and Marsyas's body, reverting now to the status

of a brute, dumb animal, went on in hopeful
disbelieving, heart thumping away in the blue furnace
of itself, lungs fighting leafy crusts (an organ,
so anatomists tell us, so wonderfully porous
it survives in the transfer from a body to another body),
tears stinging his flittered cheeks, for a full
half turning of the sundial before darkness came

upon him, and he curled into position like a dog.

Miriam Gamble

SHHHH...

Unlike McSquirter,
who sprayed
like some juvenile delinquent
the walls
of my parents' house
with his filthy water,
his gang culture
proprietorial
YAH!!

he takes the gentleman's approach:
silk-stockinged,
offering
a canapé, or can he take
your coat?
he will ply one cheek
and then the other
to your witless trouser-leg,
a Judas,
claiming you as
his own;

imparts
with his kisses
a short, sharp stink
of pheromone
to oculate skins,
the enemy
of terriers
and priestesses –
riders of that border zone
which at night
he girds
his domain against, cheeking up
the windows,
raising his hackles
silently
to neither flesh nor bone.

Gina Ferrara

WHEN YOU ARRIVE

I am indigenous with no desire to leave.
Layers of my skin surrender
and become the soft terrain between trees.
My dialect buckles distinct as an ancient root.
The scintillating blade glimmers
and swoops steadfast to clear a path.
I hear it shearing thickets, palmettos, reeds,
centuries of entanglement.
Sunlight barely penetrates canopies,
or the union of limbs.
Beyond the cleft I will be found
standing on mounds of berries and graves
offering all that's left in my hand.

Aidan Rooney

THE WHISPERING GALLERY AT GRAND CENTRAL

Into one corner outside The Oyster Bar
you closed your eyes and whispered just one prayer.

It shot across the archway like a star
then back to you because no one was there.

Howard Wright

SOUTH CITY
 – *for Geraldine*

The sunlight on Dawson Street coerced us into bookshops,
and along Grafton Street humanity flowed like money making money.
But fearing the Georgian bricks would utter Georgian poetry,
I would rather have us staying in these Europhile suburbs

in a cut-price room at the vanishing point on the perspective
of an overlit corridor in an international hotel, corporate and discreet,
if barely serviceable for lovers raucous with drink in lives
that have found a middle and stay there, you out like a light

in a flutter of biorhythms, and me the insomniac so shallow in
my sleep I'm suffocating with hindsight and alert to the winds
and rain clenching the long windows as a cold front grinds
down reprocessing plants and radioactive tides of an ocean

arrayed with early-warning hyper-sensitive microphones
which could register our shift from peevish café of passive smoke
to Hartigan's snug, Hourican's high chairs to the newspaper kiosk
on Fitzwilliam and Leeson (another perspective) all the phones

that rang at once inferring what brought us back to the fair city
was simply escape. In the twenty years of letdowns and bad faith
of this eternal student, taking an open boat across the Liffey
was my one act of bravado. When you were spiking your quiff

I was hiding (no, wasting time) in Ranelagh coveting a Clyde Road
    wife
in the midday magic of Herbert Park; you had found a cause
and fought for it, so now when you sleep easy the reason is your life,
parallel, if not tangential, to my own... Victim of seasickness

(perhaps it has always been a fear of water) I steady myself
against you, my horizon, even as I'm stung by the infra-red sniper dot
of the tv on standby, and hearing the storm, slip from your heat,
and stumble buck-naked across the wishy-washy carpet to cleave

the blurry curtains with a heavy hand and contemplate the present
and constant fears beyond the smeared windows and immobilisers
twinkling in the carpark below, the rain in buckets, the flats opposite,
and the skyline away to the north of a city beautiful in all weathers.

Howard Wright

SCRAP

Not in townlands mistranslated into polythene hay bales,
giant bowling-ball pirns of hay coming to rest between Tandragee
and Jerretspass; not behind the tumbled wall of Drumbanagher,
the defaced pitches at Tyrone's Ditches and Laurelvale,

all those flag-flying farmlands jittery with freshwater sparkle
that deserve something better (for are we not peacemakers?).
Better turn off this metalled B-road and go round the back,
through scabious and electric fences and what is left.

You may have to hurt yourself to evidence the top of a gable
jutting from the meta-geological cross-section of plastic and steel
crushed and piled in towers of scrap, a techno-archaeology
of exo-skeletons dead as Henry Ford, his son Edsel,

tail-fins and chrome bumpers, the sidewall of a breaker's yard,
the iceberg-tip of which is patched, sealed, undercoated,
and consummately decorated in generous full-scale
copper-plate: *HANDBUILT WINGS A SPECIALITY.*

Susie DeCoste

AFTER ATTEMPTING SUICIDE, AFTER A WEEKEND SNEAK-OUT TO HUNT RABBIT ALONE

Slice round the ankles and up the belly
to get the skin from the meat.
By now you've cut off the head, of course,
then peel. Like a good orange,
it will come off in one piece.

I chew the little rabbit pieces
curled up and dark as if ready for sleep,
blanketed by sinister carrots, onions.
Cider coaxes them down my throat.

Spread their wings under
your feet, hold them steady,
partridges are easy too.
By now you've twisted off the head, of course,
tossed it under a tree. Then pull
up on the feet, the carcass slides right out.

A crunchy bit, too hard for bone.
I swallow pieces of my molar and a tiny black ball.

To avoid pellets in the meat, you shoot the head.
But I missed, got his ears shooting on the run.
I knew he would
                    drop sooner or later.

Daniel Hardisty

MERMAID ALIVE

On the third day she was still alive,
caked in Saxo salt,
her carp arms jewelled with peacock eyes.
I began to hope.
Her shallow breathing like the gentle
lapping of water in the sinkbowl.
A compass needle dropped in her hand
would now swing north.
My cheap cotton towels wrung and re-soaked
and laid again along her dried tail.
The wire grill of scales
slowly finding their lustre.

She slept.
I watched her like daft Narcissus in the pool.
Only she was my other self.
Wiping the salt foam of her lips:
a silver fish flashed in the
black bowl of her eye.
I would live.

Daniel Hardisty

ELEGY
after Pushkin

Drunk my whole glorious Twenties
I look back now and know that was
the high watermark and this is the hangover. The pain
of it ripens like wine in its hourly bottle.
The path ahead is dry. Tomorrow is dry!
The future is like no ocean; it is work
and unhappiness.

Poets, I am too selfish to want to die –
there's enough even in living and suffering.
Something in this menu of puritanical fare
must whet the appetite; and anyway isn't 'suffering',
'pain', 'unrequited love' the roughage
of our so-called daily bread?
Besides it's not as if the bars
have closed their doors forever;
doesn't love still nod somewhere with a saluting drink,
or a parting smile?

Enda Coyle-Greene

GRACE

The door's closing was an exhaled breath caught
between worlds, the heft of a feather overheard
      above the engine, a balm

to calm the heart-rate that the monitor kept its trace
on through the tick, tick boom of the box attached
      to my waist,

the snake of rubber rope around my neck, the cuff
that flinched and finished in the tightness of a vice-
      bite on my arm

on the half-hour, every half-hour. I'd remembered,
in the intervening minutes, to allow the day to go
      right over me

before the panic started by the held-until-my-hand-
hurt inhalation died, and I could breathe again.
      On Grafton Street, it happened

and on Westland Row, I timed it on the way to Pearse;
there, the platforms, northbound, southbound,
      jittered,

other travellers, speeding up for effect, fast-forwarded
like a film when the action bucks and jolts
      as required by the story.

The train pulled in and I got on, turned left and sat
beside the window, hoped I could be quiet, hoped
      I'd be invisible.

His height, when he appeared, absorbed the light
as he sat down in front of me. I don't know why
      I thought

he took two seats. His body was a clash of angles,
seemed to be as long and thin as his black tie,
      his shirt was white,

his hair, another, softer white, a buzz-cut flare
above a face that wasn't old, but wasn't young.
      He put his briefcase down

between his knees that almost, almost but not quite,
touched mine, there was the sudden clarity of grey-
      sky eyes,

the cool surprise of when he spoke and said,
I'm glad I got this one – when I said,
      Yes,

there's quite a gap between them at this time
of day – that I had answered him. I checked
      my phone

and saw that it was coming up to three o'clock.
I waited as the train drew nearer to a station
      I, perhaps, imagined

he had mentioned, wondered if he'd say goodbye,
if I would nod, or smile; instead, I kept my head
      inside my book

as I was gripped. Waiting on that too to pass,
I didn't see him leave. Next morning, in the surgery,
      the readouts told

a story of a day, a night, my heart-beat's crush of blood:
It's very high, the doctor said, *It's uniform, except –*
      just look –

you'll see – and pointing to the stitch of times
as jagged mountains, then, to where the difference
      was defined –

a flatter line – she looked again and asked me
once, just once, where I had been the day before,
      at three.

Nicholas Bradley

LETTER TO THEO

The work? I work so fast, sweat at the harvest.
Times, tobacco-dizzy, as the sun shrieks,
I fetch an emptiness, the limp head pounds.

Around they gather, whispering to disinfect,
the shadows that discuss me, posthumous.

But then, O heavens, it comes back
like sulphur to my tongue,
the deity of day re-scored
and wild horse rollicking in blood.

Again the orchard shines
with apple blossom, pure,
and morning, O sweet morning, breaking in my veins.

I see spiders on their webs of breath
and feel my thumb-hold, whale's eye, pulse.

Step into life,
long grass and butterflies draw near;
I hear their murmur when the screaming stops.

Sam Gardiner

DEVIL'S COACH-HORSE

Head eclipsing the horizontal sun,
her hair streams fire, blue breath rises
from the small furnace at her lips
and both ears glow translucent red.
'Why don't you come round and try again,'
she murmurs from within her skin-tight
black leather outfit, as there draws out
from beneath the seaside bench
we sit on, a Devil's Coach-Horse,
a large old-fashioned beetle
in wet-look purple-black livery.
Miniscule silver eyes gleaming she
approaches my pitch-black boot and arches
her posterior enticingly, or in mockery.
You can never tell with beetles.

Sam Gardiner

THE CANDLEBLOWER'S RECITER

From here to there is signposted through
Happyland Amusement Park, which leads a life
of its own, past a chapelful of candles
and an ivied stump not far from Coleraine,
where a reddish beetle pretends to be unpalatable,
until a grey crow is completely not fooled.

But there are ways of going nowhere
beyond all time for leaving, and staying to see
someone swing past with rook-rifle and sack
in which the ducks she has blinded for decoys
cry out from permanent night,
unrelieved by even a candelabrum of stars.
All great mysteries begin with a death.

How to get there from here requires a sail
round the globe on simple sailcloth,
single-(meaning two-)handed, or one short step
backwards off a high roof like young Elpenor
without the Olympian hangover but grasping
a rusted aerial bracket. Or frequent, if furtive,
recourse to The Candleblower's Reciter.

Many a bankrupt, heedless of the flats above,
who left a candle burning in a tub of margarine,
and pretended not to know the time
in a selection of pubs well out of town,
owes his freedom to the Candleblower.

Others may be afraid of their secret thoughts.
They condemn themselves because they failed
to spot the camera when they loitered or fled,
touched wood, left fingerprint, voice print,
or DNA which is being analysed as we speak.

And do you abase yourself the better to climb,
pray for injustice and use virtue to blackmail?
Or perhaps we both count on the Candleblower
extinguishing unworthy wishes and intentions
before the canopy catches fire and burns
the sky, brings it floating down in black flakes
that erase every track and pathway.

Sam Gardiner

FEET (A CORONET)

1
Personally I'm thrilled that a Magdalene
could wash His feet in Chanel No 5
and towel them with a curtain
of hair, and this was fine.

2
Fine feet for nailing, to the true wood
for murder by carpentry, when it fails
to convert a dead tree to
a cornice of dovetails.

3
Tailored camomile lawns patrolled
by aphoristic gnomes, themselves metaphors
for excremental toads' stools,
are marqueed by sycamores.

4
The more they clipped the angels' wings
the stronger they grew the higher to fly;
the more the lanthorn swang
the less it scried thereby.

5
By striking lengthwise along the roofs
sunlight shrinks the autocracy of frost
to isosceles being schooled
in the geometry of corners.

6
Cornered by congruity, to test and turn
and try to jettison the capsule
you were cast adrift in,
seems incongruous not to.

7
Not to conform seems callous when she
has de-crusted her heels and gold-leafed
her toenails, with an asymmetry
I find thrilling, personally.

Sam Gardiner

HANDS (A CORONET)

1
Hand in hand on a vandalised bench in
the Garden of Remembrance, inseparable
while his name remains
hers on the marble slab.

2
A slab-sided gelatinous coagulum
in a tank, octopus blinks an oceanic
eye and votes for freedom
with a show of hands.

3
Hands prickling with pins and needles
she looks unstricken, still knows a trick
or two. A concrete Venus
is not the girl to panic.

4
Panicking the air, the magpie's wings try
their hand at opposing circles; instead of
tearing apart, it flies off
by artful compromise.

5
Compromised by convolvulus (the genus
of the place), in a tented bank
where she felt the first stars
tremble in her hand.

Christina Park

DOG LOVE

Our love is dog love
      No question

Of complication – what if, or how – just
This

Animal-eye love, and never mind
      Will you, won't you, just

The everything that it means, falling
      Onto the grass together, laughing, panting.
Sunshine, the warmth of my hand in your pelt. This
Is dog love,
      What we'd call innocence

If we knew better.

Mark Roper

HALCYON

My mother had a very strong need to be outside, in the fresh air, using
her body. She loved to walk, to swim, to play tennis, to row. It wasn't a
case of her feeling she ought to take exercise, the need ran much deeper:
it was a fundamental part of her nature, something independent, solitary,
even wild in her, something which had to go its own way, outside.

When she came to visit us in Ireland, she'd often go for a walk if we
were out at work, through the wood opposite our house, Gortrush
Wood. It's a conifer wood, at that time about forty years old: the trees
were spread well apart, there was room for other kinds of trees to grow
in between them. It was a walk we'd grown very fond of.

One day when we got back from work she told us, excitedly, that she
had seen a kingfisher on her walk, on a small pool at the edge of the wood.
This pool was actually more a long shallow puddle, where rainwater
would collect in a hollow between trees. It was brackish, and would all
but dry out in the summer. It was a long way from any reasonably-sized
stream. It had nothing in the way of a bank. It surely couldn't have
contained any fish. For all these reasons I was quite convinced that she
must have been mistaken, she couldn't possibly have seen a kingfisher
there.

Over the years that followed, I used to tease her about this, linking it
to her general vagueness about the animal kingdom. This was a woman,
after all, who had only just discovered that elephants didn't eat through
their trunks. It became a shared joke. We'd send each other cards with
kingfishers on, cuttings from newspapers about them. One of us would
pretend suddenly to see the bird, in the most unlikely setting. It was a
shared joke, but it also became a kind of shared tenderness. Slowly a
kingfisher began to come alive, to appear between us. When she came to
the first poetry reading of mine that she was able to attend, I saw she
was wearing a medallion with a kingfisher on it. It was quite a large
medallion, made of pewter, on a long metal chain, quite ostentatious in
its way – not the sort of thing she wore normally at all.

A few years after her claimed sighting, the wood was cut, and replanted
in the modern way, the trees very close to each other. Now that they've
grown a bit, it's impossible to walk there. But, for a few years before the
new trees grew, I continued to do so, and one day I realised that every
time I approached the pool, I was looking for the kingfisher. I was quite
sure my mother hadn't seen one, sure that in fact she couldn't have seen
one there, but all the same I was expecting to see one. In this way too,
the bird had come alive.

At some point, the line 'I've never seen the kingfisher' came into my head. Poems often start this way for me, a line cropping up, a line with some kind of ring to it, around which other lines might eventually start to cohere. I didn't know what to do with this line, but it was there, and one day I discovered that the word *Kingfisher* is linked to the word *Halcyon*. I knew the phrase *Halcyon Days*, days of idyllic happiness or prosperity: my dictionary told me that *Halcyon* came from the Greek word for kingfisher, *Alkuon* or *Halcuon*, from *Hals* meaning sea, and *Kuon* meaning conceiving. I consulted my *Brewer's Dictionary of Phrase and Fable*, where I found *Kuon* translated as 'to brood on'. Brewer's added: 'The ancient Sicilians believed that the kingfisher laid its eggs, and incubated them for fourteen days on the surface of the sea, during which period, before the winter solstice, the waves were always unruffled.'

My father had died some twenty years earlier, and my mother had mourned him deeply. Suddenly I began to see a connection between the word *Halcyon* and her situation. I saw that 'to brood on' could mean both to breed, to conceive, but also to think deeply about something, often in a melancholy way. I went on to look up the word in Robert Graves's *The Greek Myths*, but I couldn't find it in the Index. Eventually it occurred to me to look it up under 'A', where I found *Alcyone* (incidentally underneath *Alcyoneus*, meaning *Mighty Ass*, which I took as a deserved rebuke for my slowness). Graves gives a fuller version of the story:

> Alcyone was the daughter of Aeolus, guardian of the winds, and Aegiale. She married Ceyx of Trachis, son of the Morning Star, and they were so happy in each other's company that she daringly called herself Hera, and him Zeus. This naturally vexed the Olympian Zeus and Hera, who let a thunderstorm break over the ship in which Ceyx was sailing to consult an oracle, and drowned him. His ghost appeared to Alcyone who, greatly against her will, had stayed behind in Trachis, whereupon distraught with grief, she leapt into the sea. Some pitying god transformed them both into kingfishers.
>
> Now, every winter, the hen-kingfisher carries her dead mate with great wailing to his burial and then, building a closely compacted nest from the thorns of the sea-needle, launches it on the sea, lays her eggs in it, and hatches out her chicks. She does all this in the Halcyon Days – the seven which precede the winter solstice, and the seven which succeed it – while Aeolus forbids his winds to sweep across the waters.

I had my poem now, about my mother, a woman who loved the sea, whose need to swim in it had been heightened by the loss of her husband, a loss she brooded on. She was still deeply united with him. In the other sense of the word 'brood', I had been part, along with my sisters, of her brood. This was the poem:

HALCYON

I've never seen the kingfisher
you claim to have witnessed
on the stand of brackish water
at the edge of our wood.

Years I've been looking.
Not a sign. Wrong habitat
too: no bank for nesting,
indeed no fish. Face it

there was no bird, yet
each time I pass I peer into
that gloom and each time
this comes to mind:

a flash of chestnutsapphire.
A small flame brooding on ooze.
Your words made light.
Your bright idea. You diving

through the long years
of grief to surface here,
halcyon, incorruptible.
And not one bird but a pair.

My mother died last autumn. Around that time, I had seen a deer vanishing into another small wood nearer to our house. This small wood faces Gortrush Wood over a large field. It's a wood of alder and willow, on wet ground, many of the trees thickly coated with lichen and moss, quite a few fallen. It's the last patch of wood left now along this stretch of road and it must be something of a refuge, a way station, for wild creatures. The deer had most likely escaped from the large agricultural college, some two miles away, where they have a deer farm, but it was still a special experience to witness it crashing into the trees.

I hadn't seen it again, but early on this year I was walking past the wood, and I realised that I was straining to see it, in just the same way that I had strained for so long to see the kingfisher that my mother couldn't have seen, in Gortrush Wood. I grinned to myself, thinking that now I would have to repeat this new pattern, looking for the deer every time I passed this spot.

At that exact moment, from the edge of the wood, where a small stream runs under the road, a kingfisher flashed up, swerved left along the road, then veered right, out across the field, heading toward Gortrush Wood where my mother claimed to have seen one so many years before.

It was an extraordinary moment, an extraordinary coincidence. The bird appeared exactly when I had been thinking about my mother and her kingfisher. And of course that made it an encounter with her, with her spirit. And then I realised that she had been right all along, here was the proof of her claim, a kingfisher in nearly the same spot. I felt a huge need to tell her, to share the news, and then I remembered that she was dead. I stood in the middle of the road and told her anyway.

I have since read that kingfishers roam widely in winter. They can be found far away from water inland, they can be found by the sea. Maybe the bird I saw lives around here, maybe it was a visitor. 'Only the righteous see the kingfisher' is a saying recorded in Mark Cocker's *Birds Britannica*. After unrighteously denying her sighting, I had been given a second chance. Why I was so sure she hadn't seen one, I don't know. But I have learnt to try to check my judgment. And I think I understand more deeply now that what we might actually witness is only a tiny fraction of what there is. I see more deeply how our thinking is formed, has always been formed, by the world around us. So much passed between my mother and me through the image of that bird. I wear the punishment for my unright-eousness lightly: condemned, whenever I pass that wood, to be on the lookout for both deer and kingfisher; condemned to try to be open to every possibility.

Darrell Epp

THE RIVER

twitching waiting for the mailman
wondering about how things change.
'you can't step in the same river twice,'
you said, because the river's constantly
changing. 'if that's true,' i said, 'you
can't step in the same river even once,
can you? it's changing as you're stepping,'
but you didn't understand what i meant
and you certainly never understood how
much i wanted to build us a treehouse
in the jungle where we could eat bananas
all day and i could beat my chest like i
was tarzan lord of the apes. and what
were you thinking anyhow, glibly quoting
heraclitus to a man with tears in his eyes?
like a dog returning to his vomit i patrol
the used bookstores, the empty cathedrals.
the sheets don't smell of you, like always.
how gone you are, how always returning.

Darrell Epp

KISSING PIRANHAS

'it's not what you *meant* to do,
it's what you *did* that i don't like'
is what you say in front of the bingo
parlour and hey, how many bingo

parlours does one downtown need?
the cars all wish they were horses.
the trains wish they were mighty
godzillas. and what do you wish?

to be a cockroach, with your bones
on the outside, your thin skin under
a hard shell? that might work better
for you than zoloft and / or placebos,

but i'm no doctor. piranhas french-
kiss in the water that's risen to my
knees but i'm not going anywhere:
everybody knows i was here first.

Carrie Etter

HOMECOMING

The train halts to a shudder.

No. The train stops. In the last car, there is no reverberation.

The man across the aisle swaggers out of his seat. 'We struck a vehicle,' he says.

The royal we, as in the train itself? Or the collective we? One hundred seventy-two passengers, ticket collector, café cashier, and engineer: we.

The verb to strike does not require a preposition of direction or movement: consider ploughed, crashed *into*: a puncturing, a violation.

A vehicle, if a body, is a vehicle for the soul or the brain and its magnificent synapses that carry all our aspirations.

We await police and fire.

The engineer walks between the rails, his footprints defined by accumulated, frozen snow.

The prints are clear close to us, but nearing the vehicle, they sink less into the white.

The swaggering man speaks with the ticket collector, who murmurs 'passed away.' 'Dead?' the man replies. 'Dead!'

At fifty yards off, the impressions disappear entirely, for as the engineer approached death, his body lightened, gravity loosening its claim.

Two hundred yards back, the car split, one half on the rails, the other spun into a snowbank through which rise brush and thistle resembling saplings, kin to the short, bare trees along the track.

We await the Cook County Coroner, after which, the collector reports, we can continue down Illinois, towards Christmas.

A young man in a university sweatshirt passes with his long-lensed camera and shares glimpses of the site, uniformed men fixed in a semi-circle.

We await an engineer to replace ours, the man standing aside, lonelier than he has ever been.

Almost every passenger holds a phone to an ear, speaks to a relative. 'Sad?' says one woman. 'Oh, yes, it's really sad.'

Three and a half hours later, the train resumes its journey. Five hours and we step away, into a last collective sigh. The station sign reads 'Normal, Illinois,' and someone – we won't look – can't stop laughing.

Fergus Allen

THE NEW KING OF THE CASTLE

The town I lived in was the small town
That surrounded me in the state of lunacy.
As a place it had always been somehow foreign,
Its people shadowy, their minds clad in burkas,
Inaccessible to my weak intuition.
At one end of the crowded high street
Rose the castle, whose privileged occupants
Were known by name, but were as alien
And unapproachable as crocodiles –
Even more so than the beings in the town.

When by the freakish outcome of a lottery
I was able to lay my hands on the castle
As well as what would count as a fortune
For myself and those I called my dependants,
My way of life became idle and pampered,
While the townspeople, the town, the castle,
Remained as distant and unexplained as ever,
Baffling me, their objective existence
Still a mystery, with no self-evident
Reason why they should be there at all.

My own thatness was just as much in doubt.
Was I the invention of those who observed me
Walking up and down the alleys of the market
And of the servants who stood respectfully aside
When I strolled along the castle's corridors?
Heels clicking on stone, I climbed a spiral
Stairway to look into what were empty rooms,
Finally peering out of the cupola
To find nothing but light – white cloud perhaps –
Undifferentiated, yielding, intangible.

Came the revolution, the people of the town,
Their heads in bandages with eye-holes,
Forced an entry to the castle and ran wild,
Their muffled cries beyond my understanding,
Though not beyond the grasp of my dependants
Who poured harum-scarum through the saloons,
Screeching like hens into whose cosy coop
A fox with a one-track mind has burst.
And when my turn came I perceived briefly
Something I guessed with confidence was pain.

Justin Quinn

MUSÍLKOVA

1.
The man was shot two bridges up the river,
an NKVD spy at work in Prague,
the German occupation hardly over.
His job was propaganda and intrigue

and contact with the local Communists.
It's hard to say exactly just what turn
events will now take, what the larger costs
of his corpse on the pavement in this yarn

I'm reading in a café two bridges down.
The novel unfolds brilliantly across
the entire continent, Prague merely one
small detail worked into the larger canvas.

The characters reduce themselves to print
when I shut the book and put it on the table.
Their world though is right here. I could walk round
to where this Russian bunked before his trouble.

They leave the oddest gaps within my day.
The coffee on the table has gone cold
and mails keep coming with more work to do
in the town where this man was never killed.

2.
One August evening out with you. Clear sky.
An art-house film theatre in a courtyard.
Apartments from the '30s stacked up high.
We had a glass outside before the start.

My smoke went floating up into the air.
A man came out onto his balcony
and lit a cigarette and drank a beer,
his cat beside him waiting patiently.

The pleasure of the evening was intense –
a sweetness of the air, the light, the glass,
light-headed in the sky's expanse.
Incredible to think that this would pass.

3.
On Saturday evening, I ride the bus
from our burb into town in rainy weather.
My nose in a book, completely oblivious,
one dream distracting me from the other,

from this, from what you might call public life:
hip to hip, eyes staring straight ahead,
the loners, lovers, the quiet man and wife,
alive with glances and small shifts of body weight.

A TV actor gets on at one stop
and everyone tries and fails not to look
at his real skin and hair, his clothes, his cap,
the obvious script he takes from his back-pack

that will project him on so many screens –
an hour's distraction from all this right here.
The bus swings down Musílkova and rounds
onto to the home straight. Two minutes we're there.

4.
Named for a local doctor, executed
in 1940 for his work in resistance.
Whether he was recruiter or recruited,
whether he placed bombs or just gave assistance,

is hard to find out now, or why he joined
when most other people were dragging their feet.
Suddenly no options left. A single point.
Led out into a yard. Became a street.

Justin Quinn

ON THE TRANSLATOR'S ART
  – for Martin Hilský

I

The woods go dark. What language and what names
Do all these shadows have that twist and rise?
Kings and asses, spirits at their games,
Monkeys, blackamoors and villains' lies;
Or lovers straying in the forest, sick
With love and hate that plays through them like fated
Rhymes and rhythms, changed in the very nick
Of seasons: they are constantly translated
By good fellows with wands, quills or machines.
They swear and dance in time. They make their vows
Then disappear in shifting flats and scenes.
The players come back out and take their bows
    Before the people underneath the flag
    Of the royal court of Athens, London or Prague.

II

Turncoats, traitors: they turn words inside out.
They know more than the critic or the theorist.
They check the stitching and the seams. Each doubt
And each decision shows they see clearest.
They are the final villains of the piece:
Look for them in one country or one nation
And these quick snakes have slipped across the crease
Between two languages: this is translation.
Such characters as Edmund and Iago
Are stalwarts of the state compared to them.
How else could Shakespeare, who is England, know
These Slavic accents, this tongue of chernozem?
    How could a stage with *Národ sobě*
    Be moved by someone with an OBE?

III

Why are they speaking English anyway –
These Danes, these Picts, these most Italian Greeks?
Why shouldn't they talk Czech as well and play
In Whitby or wherever England speaks
Most purely and most clearly from the source?
What source is not a multilingual mud?
How great and deep is England without recourse
To Roman, Swedish, French and Irish blood?
Without the US – Rome to England's Greece –
Where you can hear Elizabethans talk
In malls and prairies? There is never any peace
In language or the world. Go for a walk
    Through Whitechapel: at stalls above the sewer
    The accents clash, making English pure.

IV

In May, the Petřín blooms and lovers go
Among its lilacs, almonds and acacias.
The words that they speak then will bloom and grow
And make their souls as generous and spacious
As the sky, as well as eddies and small changes
In the denotations and the connotations
Of those words spoken, lip to ear; their ranges
Enlarged in part for these new generations
By plays that are translated summer dreams.
Across the hill, Shakespeare Open Air
Continues in Prague Castle. The action seems
To even catch our Hal within its glare.
    And in the trees, the songs of love and death
    Shift slightly in an altered gaze, a breath.

Justin Quinn

COUPLE

They sat there side by side: a homeless man,
a not-so-homeless looking woman, talking.
Or he was talking, mumbling on and on
at her blank face, impassive, wholly lacking

expression or the smallest ghost of it,
unless you count the stitches freshly sown
up from her eyebrow, along her forehead's height,
made redder by the paleness of her skin.

His face was folds of dirt and tan and grit,
impossible to see beyond these to
a person, though perhaps her gift was that
she saw a man in this man's residue.

A sort of couple locked into each other
and shunted through the city, oblivious
to buildings, festivals and road-work clutter.
It seemed they'd ride out to the terminus

most likely so they could avoid the cold.
His drawl – his gravelled, drunken, ageing drawl –
sank down to nothing as the tram rolled
to a stop at what you could call Bum Grand Central.

Knowing him was loving him? Or:
why not take down a large bag from a shelf
and just walk out on him, but not before
telling him that now he could fuck himself?

How we like to give out good advice
to people who so clearly need it and
might change, get happy, stop being so nice
or bored or brain-dead to the bitter end.

He slept. She tried to wake him with some pokes.
But he was really gone. She left him there
deep in his dream of drink or sex or smokes.
No hesitation. Went straight out the door.

I was left with his stink and parasites
another fifteen minutes. It wasn't good.
The city streaming by. Don't give advice.
Don't even let it flicker in your head.

John F Deane

SNOW FALLING ON CHESTNUT HILL
  Denn alles Fleisch es ist wie Gras...

It is late now in the day; that curving lane
with grass and plantain, clovers and pimpernels
forming a hump along the centre, seems
to be straightening towards a conclusion. I have arrived

in a strange city, evening; (I am hearing
Brahms, the German Requiem, *Selig sind...*blessed
are they who mourn):
Boston. A big house, and daunting.

They have warned me of arctic chill
reaching this way, over Canada, the lakes, Chicago;
*Herr, lehre doch mich...*I have heard already
oboe-moans through the eldering house, thin

reed-sounds through unseen interstices: O Lord
make me aware of my last end.
The hollow spaces of the house
are stirred along their dust: All flesh, the music tells,

is grass. I listened, dozing gently, silence,
sweet, encompassing, holding me;
at the front door I heard...
(no matter, it is no matter). I stood

watching first snow-flakes
visible against the street-lamps; there was the feel
as of the breathing on my face of a lover, as of the brush
of a kiss, sheer

arctic salt, a hosting. *Wir haben hier
keine bleibene Statt...*
All flesh
is snow. And snow

does not abide. *Selig sind die Toten*, blessed
are the dead; they are at rest
in the Lord's hands. I slept
fitfully; strange

land, strange house, strange dreams; time
raddling me. I could hear
the sound of the deepest night
lying still under a delicate coming down of snow.

*

I have been wondering
about our blizzards of pain and agony – Lupus, for instance,
immune systems down and civil war along the blood.
Prance of the alpha wolf. Bone

scaffolding showing through.
I lay unsleeping; my temporary home
whispered to itself in house-language, its wooden shifts
of consonants, its groaning vowels, when there came (Christ!)

a sudden rapping
against the door. I listened. Again,
rapping, urgent. I crept down. Opened,
I had to, street door, screen-door. Saw

darkness active out there, snow
swirling, a shape that
formed and faded out of the skirl of white and grey...
And she came, breathless,

shaking snow from her hair and face, stomping her feet,
stood in the non-light of the hallway and snow
pooled about her shoes. She, dressed in white,
reached to drop – 'a gift,' she said – one

bright Christmas rose, helleborus,
white-petalled, dark-green-leaved,
across the hallstand.
'You!' I whispered. 'You?'

She smiled.
'But we laid you down decades ago,' I said, 'to rest.'
'Isn't it good,' she said,
'to hear the crunch, under your feet, of fresh snow?'

'You are...in body, then?' 'Soul
and body, body and soul. No longer flawed.
I passed where snow is a swarm of whitest butterflies
though I had been growing old with the wolves.'

'And why? Why now? And how... ?'
'I bring,' she answered, 'gifts. Wolves too, wolves,'
she whispered, 'wolves are the lambs of God.'
'Our child,' I tried, 'is wrapped up tight in pain, God's ways...'

(I saw, then, the wolf-pack, *canis lupus*, settling under trees,
they lie easy in the snow, you can hear their howl-songs,
clarinet-calls off-key in the moon-enlightened night, drawn-
out off-melodies, lauds chanted to the blood, their green-lit
white-shaded eyes sweeping across the heavens; *canis lupus*,
grey-grizzled ancients of days, the black, the white, the gorgeous
fur and in the distance I heard the freight-train howl of human
hungers, a tailed-off threatening horn-call across the night; wolf-
pelt, winter-pelt, the scars, the tissues, and always snow falling
down the everyvein of air)

'Be peacefilled now,' she said, softly as a brushing-by of snow,
'live happily in the swing of rainfall, in the rush
of the arctic wind. We are all
sunlight, dimmed, all snowfall, thawed.'

'Our child...'
But she was already moving towards the door, her head
shaking; 'All flesh is frost
and I have been a wolf, subtle in the snow,

a lover, singing against the moon,
a lamb...' The door... I felt the touch of pre-dawn frost,
heard snow begin to slide in fistfuls from the trees,
'Wolves, too,' she said, 'wolves

are the lambs of God.'
'Wait !' I called, and reached
for her. But she was gone,
suddenly, and there was nothing, 'I have

questions...prayers...'
Silence, only, and absence. I heard still
the breathing of the snow, a car somewhere
climbing a hill. I stood in darkness. Stood. Perplexed,

as always. A snow-plough passed, the steel blades
scraping against the roads. Soon
cars, roof-racked with snow, would shift
like herds of caribou

down the long parkway. The first
faint light of a new day
touched the window. I saw,
on the hallstand, fresh and beautiful,

one hellebore, one Christmas rose.
I closed my eyes against the dawn and heard
Brahms again: *Wie lieblich sind die Wohnungen...*
how beautiful your dwellings, Lord, how beautiful.

Gerard Smyth

FATHER TO POETS, LOVER OF SONGS: JAMES LIDDY, 1934-2008

James Liddy, poet, essayist, maverick, bohemian, teacher, literary editor,
outsider, raconteur, magus, merrymaker, gossip, subversive, intellectual
explorer – and occasionally all at the same time – had the knack of becoming poet-in-residence wherever he set up camp.

In any literary conclave enlivened by his presence he became the centre
of gravity. His conversation was always eloquent, witty, entertaining. His
Wildean streak of flamboyance and expansive personality, as well as his
sense of mischief, may at times have masked the deep erudition (Flann
O'Brien in a review of Liddy's first publication, *Esau, My Kingdom for a
Drink*, seemed more concerned with the poet's 'eructation'). That erudition
came out of one of the most inquisitive and acquisitive of minds. How
true, the description of him in the homily given at his funeral Mass, as a
'collector of arcane knowledge'.

That 'arcane knowledge' was widely and joyfully shared: in the pub
corner, in his hand-written correspondence of which there must be vast
volumes for some future editor to gather, and in the classroom where his
students were treated to incisive, if unconventional, critiques of the Irish
literary tradition and the Beat poets to whom he remained a loyal and
scholarly champion.

He also remained true to Kavanagh. And to Mandelstam, Baudelaire,
Whitman, Jack Spicer, Michael Hartnett, all those spiritual brothers who
hovered over any literary conversation with James.

Inevitably, too, the ghosts of his patriot heroes would be invoked: Parnell,
John and Willie Redmond, Liam Mellows and always, always, the icon of
his heart, Michael Collins. He must have been a precociously keen observer
as a child – his recollection of de Valera's black-and-white Ireland of the
1940s were recounted with vivid actuality. The trips to the Shelbourne
Hotel with his mother and sister, Nora, where they encountered the
waiter who claimed to be Hitler's cousin, meetings with W B's widow
George Yeats, the last Ivy Day parade to the Parnell monument in
O'Connell Street.

The literary and political eras of the past haunted his imagination,
yet he was more in touch with the present than some of the young
acolytes who surrounded him. And there was always an entourage of
acolytes, attentive to the anecdotes, the remembrances, the tutorials
delivered, as if it were part of some kind of priestly function. In these
gatherings he was open, alert and loved the heat from a good argument.

He arrived in the United States, as he later said himself, on a 'mission
to meet the good poets'. American received a ready-made authority on

its own counter-culture. He joined with the Beats in their rejection of the academic template, taking to heart Jack Spicer's declaration in his 'Letter to Lorca', that the poem is 'a collage of the real'. Before landing in the midst of America's campus revolts of the Sixties, his never-forgotten evenings of initiation and discourse with Kavanagh in Dublin's literary temple of that time, McDaid's, had been a prep course for the journey outward.

If Kavanagh was his mentor, he in turn became mentor to the next generations. He was generous in his own encouragement of young writers, always making a place for them in the alternative literary journals he created or over which he had influence, the most influential of which was *Arena* in Dublin in the 1960s, but also *The Gorey Detail* in the 1970s, and latterly *The Blue Canary* in Milwaukee. Hartnett was spot on in his poem 'The Poet as Saint', when he wrote:

> He is father to many poets
> and he is lover of their songs.

The fusion of his openly gay sexuality, his Irishness and Catholicism made him a poet who defied categorisation. He formulated his own distinctive vernacular out of what he learned from Kavanagh and the Beats. What Ashbery said of Frank O'Hara, that he ignored the rules of poetry, could equally apply to James's poems, which absorbed the whole life and a world that extended from Corca Bascinn, Coolgreany and Croghan Kinsella, the mountain under which he is now buried, to his adopted German-Polish city in the American Midwest. It was there he built up a reputation as a poet of originality and style, and developed a highly regarded Irish studies programme in the University of Wisconsin-Milwaukee.

Although he took himself away from Ireland, first to become a child of the American bop night in San Francisco and New Orleans, where he enjoyed what he called a life of 'blissful Bohemian excess', and then happily go native in Milwaukee, he kept the homeland in his sights and thoughts, returning annually to celebrate his birthday among old friends and pick up the news about the latest literary intrigue or political dog-fight. His final visit took place last July with no sense that this would be the occasion for a final parting glass.

He will be missed from his nooks of old poetry – in Grogan's Lounge, Rafferty's pub and Axel's bar.

First published in *The Irish Times*, 24 November 2008.

James Liddy

'I DREAMT I DWELT IN MARBLE HALLS'

My dream in the roots, curlew sound a café –
drifting with some I know. Tom Moore's lilt
packed curlew-plaintive marble-cold... Post-dream
trauma comes: no more listening, songs will have
travelled the floor, gone through the walls.

Shall I swim the dark route under the waning
lighthouse to the Isle of Man, the island of dogs?
Then I remember father's Peugeot on another coast,
I braked the car to hunt for bits of songs; curlews
began intoning through Corca Bascinn's mist.

Under the sea wall down to Philip II's sunken
liberation galleon, the sounds kept me marooned
all August nights in Kilkee: loneliness so still
such is the kingdom of souls. The region's music
escorts of the dead commingled sea and seaweed...

I remember mother's brown bread and oysters
in The Red Bank, I remember Lord Wicklow's
whiskey brown bread oysters in the Bailey,
Kavanagh and Anne Yeats also there. Anne's
questions, 'Mr Liddy, would you like another

gin and soda?' I held my glass towards that estate.

James Liddy

I write from Ivy Court Inn & Suites.
A hot boring kid I wore an ivy leaf
in my lapel in Coolgreany wood,
surrounded by these three other skins,
romance, rebellion, realism.
You foraged each expanding excelsis.
Alright blessed be Avondale tree leaves.

When I was a boy with bread and butter in my heart.

It's been raining all day in this town.
Rain dropped on Hosiers outside my heart.
Out the hotel window I watch a sign –
Irish Import Shop, I get Crunchie bars,
McVities biscuits, and a red button
'I survived an Irish Catholic Childhood.'
Eric says, 'You didn't survive it.'

When I was a boy with bread and butter in my heart.

My hot bones are not yet weary
to downtown graduate student Guinness,
but tonight's juice was God in
exile in the chatter and change.
Ivy leaf jumps to Coolgreany wood
to my green core vow. Come God or
fairies, deal us the cards we can play.

When I was a boy with only bread and butter in my heart.

James Liddy

A NEARY'S AFTERNOON

There's Barry Fitzgerald hunched in the corner
with his silver top cane, he buys one drink,
sips the rest of the afternoon from what's
under the silver head. That's Siobhan
MacKenna, a clutch of theatre owls –
she'll make them rotten with drink,
turn them out later from her Rathgar house.

Salad days in the hostelry of the Golden Fleece.

A nice man comes in, Con Levental, tailored,
coiffeured, less Bloom light than Trinity air
either way a street cloud in Dublin. I whisper
how honorable to sell *Ulysses* under
the counter in a pissed Guinness puritan
town – he's off to Paris for Sam's beck and call,
we return to the beautiful nests we have made.

Gold sun down on them as they barge café doors.

We say how extravagant it is to choose avatars –
Joyce in his chain-charms of alcohol, Con's
Parisian in colonial chains of less Alcohol.
Clairvoyant modernism costs a lot, we put
on war-weary paint. Padraic Fallon from Wexford
bow-tied joins the table. He doesn't want me
here, who's been telling thespian tales?

Around a corner McDaid's dome under heaven.

James Liddy

VERSES FOR THE BELMULLET FESTIVAL

The grey-green bog drives the fire
the wind nudges flares in clouds
nothing is implausible in a place
abandoned from time to time.

Eileen O'Casey talked to me in
a Milwaukee Chinese restaurant:
her parents had the Belmullet hotel,
a chorus girl in London she danced
with the Prince of Wales (Windsor),
'He wasn't much of a man,
in a abandoned moment I asked,
"David, would you like to visit
Belmullet in the Spring incognito,"
he smiled upwards at the idea.'
Band and dance faded into silence.

Colour parades through the bog like
a pennant, lavender and bog cotton.
If you believe in happiness make
an implausible gesture towards it.

The four poems published here were sent by James Liddy from his home in
Milwaukee to the editor of *Poetry Ireland Review* on 16 October 2008. James
Liddy passed away on 4 November 2008.

Richard Murphy

TEA WITH OLIVER ST JOHN GOGARTY, RENVYLE, 1951

This is the text of Richard Murphy's address (recorded in Sri Lanka) to this year's Oliver St John Gogarty Literary Festival at Renvyle House Hotel, Connemara, Co Galway.

I thank Joan McBreen and Zoe Coyle for inviting me to participate in the Oliver St John Gogarty Festival at Renvyle this weekend, and I am sorry that my age of eighty-one has prevented me attending. Greetings to you all, and especially to my friends and fellow speakers – I am missing you – Gerald Dawe, Nuala Ní Dhomhnaill, Michael O'Loughlin, John O'Donnell and Nicola Gordon Bowe. I am living in retirement in the ancient Buddhist city of Kandy in the central highlands of Sri Lanka, too far from Ireland to face the journey at this time of year. But I still have a voice that can travel.

Never having written about Gogarty, and with no books at hand, I must rely on imagination as well as memory in telling you about my one and only meeting with the mischievous, affable, quick-witted, ever so entertaining and sadly bitter old man in the Renvyle House Hotel. He was seventy-three years old, renowned for his friendship with Yeats, who had included him in the *Oxford Book of Modern Verse*, but embittered by Joyce's comic portrayal of him as the stately, plump Buck Mulligan in the opening pages of *Ulysses*.

I was fifty years younger than Gogarty, and the time was the radiant summer of 1951. Aged twenty-three, I had 'chucked up everything' in London, such as reviewing poetry for the *Spectator*, 'and just cleared off', as the poet Larkin was to write a little later. I had gone to live alone in a cottage built before the Great Famine as a coastguard station beside the quay of Rosroe on the Big Killary, nine miles from where you are sitting. The tide reached up to a wall six feet from my bedroom window. The nearest well was across a barbed wire fence at a mud-hole in a field of rushes and rocks.

My neighbours were fishermen, shepherds and subsistence farmers, who didn't bother with books other than *Whitaker's Almanac*. Perhaps they regarded books as 'a dull and endless strife', as Wordsworth had written, or, in the words of Philip Larkin, when he was Librarian at the University of Hull, 'a load of crap'. I wanted to write an epic poem, against the grain of modern poetry, at a time when narrative verse was utterly unfashionable, the novel having replaced it. I had published no more than one poem in each of *The Irish Times*, *Envoy* and *The Bell*. What had brought me to Rosroe, at the back of beyond, was my astonishing luck, as an unheard-of dark horse running against the favourite, Anthony Cronin, in winning the AE Memorial Award of £100 given in Dublin every five years to a poet under thirty.

That was enough for me to sign a five-year lease at £20 a year on the Quay House at Rosroe, simply furnished with iron beds and horse-hair mattresses, deal tables and kitchen chairs. A few years earlier, so I was told, the house had been briefly occupied by a German writer, who had encouraged the birds to eat out of his hand, but made them so tame in a few months that when he left they were gobbled up by the village cats. Later I learned that this legend was inspired by Wittgenstein, the philosopher, who had been working at Rosroe on his *Philosophical Investigations*. In 1956, after my lease expired, the cottage would be sold to the Irish Youth Hostel Association, to become known as the Killary Youth Hostel, attracting crowds of young people to cheer up that lonely sad place.

With neither a telephone nor a car nor a wireless, and the nearest stop on the Galway-Leenane-Clifden bus route six miles across the hill and around two lakes, I depended for news on the postman, who came, wet or dry, from Renvyle. It took him all day, on a bicycle draped in yellow oil-cloth, as he had to stop and read some of the letters from abroad to people who lacked the ability. It must have been in June that he told me the owner of the Renvyle House Hotel, Dr Gogarty, who had written books, had returned from America, and it would not be a waste of my time to go and meet him, as he was a great talker, he could make a cat laugh.

The chance of meeting a man who had been a friend of the poet I most revered, W B Yeats, whose *Collected Poems* I had recently reviewed, was worth the effort of walking and cycling, avoiding puddles in potholes on the gravel road that wound up and down the hills along the weepingly beautiful coast from Salruck through Lettergesh and Tully Cross to Renvyle. In those days, only one bungalow marred the beauty of that coast, or relieved the relentless boredom, whichever way you like to look at it. And that fine afternoon, the only cars I may have passed would have belonged to Father Luddon at Tully Cross or Dr Flynn at Letterfrack or my grand-aunt Violet Barber at Salruck House. The only tractors I might have heard would have been bringing turf home from the bog.

Three years earlier, I had met Oliver St John Gogarty's son, who was running the hotel – can you believe this? – unprofitably, with a bar in the basement that he kept open, late into the night, for what were called 'bona fide travellers' and one or two carousing residents, reputed to be 'idle rich' or 'rotten with money'. One of these, I remember, was an English lordly remittance man, who never removed the shades from his eyes. But now, I had heard, the writer's wife had taken control and was running the hotel herself, with no late night drinking but still at a loss.

There was not a guest to be seen when I arrived, hot and nervous, but one or two might have been out fishing for salmon or sea trout on the lakes and rivers. Mrs Gogarty met me at the front door, and invited me to wait a while for her to find her husband and bring us tea. When Gogarty appeared, old and grey but far from sleepy, he looked neither stately nor plump, but sprightly and thin, quick and alert in his eyes, talking so fast and so well that he put me at my ease. No need to risk saying something stupid that might have provoked a clever mocking Dubliner's reply, whose wits had been sharpened by Joyce. All I had to do was listen and smile.

His wife came and went, leaving us alone with the tea things on the table. Having passed me the scones, Gogarty intoned:

' "The butter is by your elbow, Father Hart" ... Great poetry, that, don't you think, Murphy?'

I grinned as if to seem to know, as he soon explained with mocking relish, that he was quoting a line of verse from an early play of Yeats called *The Land of Heart's Desire*.

Take heart, those of you who might be attending a poetry workshop at this Festival. Don't be afraid of writing rubbish. Yeats did, and in the end managed, by working hard, which genius requires, to turn rubbishy magic into magical poetry.

At the table, I remember, and what harm if I am inventing a story about a man who loved invention, Gogarty told me how, in a cycle race, (was it in the Phoenix Park?) he managed to get level on a sharp corner with the rider who was sure to win, and make him fall off his bike by saying something that gave him a shock. Sorry, I have forgotten what it was he said, and I cannot imagine. It's gone through the sieve of memory. No matter – the champion fell and Gogarty won by his wit.

After tea, he took me to the cottage where he was staying in the garden. A fire of damp turf was smouldering in the fire place. We settled comfortably into armchairs, and his monologue resumed, bitter about Joyce the scrounger and his highly undeserved reputation. Gogarty enjoyed the chance of revenge that longevity had given him to denigrate Joyce on the lecture circuits in America. Not a bad way of living, he suggested, provided you weren't cheated by agents and publishers, who were mostly dishonest. 'Mock mockers after that...' I heard in the voice of Yeats, but my memory may have been infected by that room's heady air of malice.

What Gogarty said about Yeats was memorable:

'Yeats had been misled by news of an operation that promised to restore his potency. He went straight over to London without telling me.

I could have warned him. When he came back to Dublin, I asked him why he had gone, and he replied, "For years I had not been able to satisfy George: now I can." Yeats was driven crazy with lust, but he thought it helped his poetry.'

Gogarty paused, as we heard footsteps ... and in silence he got up, seized the tongs, and pulled a few burning sods of turf out on to the hearth, filling the room with smoke.

'My wife hates smoke,' he said. 'Now we will not be disturbed.'

– Kandy, Sri Lanka, 6 November 2008

First published in *The Irish Times*, 6 December 2008.

Thomas Kilroy

REMEMBERING AUSTIN CLARKE

The following text is the speech delivered by Thomas Kilroy at the launch of Austin Clarke: Collected Poems *on Wednesday, 26 November 2008 in Newman House, 85-86 St Stephen's Green South, D2.*

Although I was in his company more than once I can't say that I ever knew Austin Clarke as such. To tell the truth, I think, as a young man, I was in awe of him.

I was present, though, at the now famous poetry reading given by Robert Frost in the old UCD Physics Theatre on Earlsfort Terrace. I remember Frost, in his acquired New England accent, declaiming his poem 'Birches'. And I remember watching the two poets after the reading, the two white heads close together behind the big bench of the theatre. What magical transmission was going on there, I wondered, poet to poet?

It was much later that I read Clarke's own account of that conversation between himself and Frost. How the American poet had asked him about the kind of poetry which he wrote. Clarke had paused for a moment, uncertain, but then he remembered a street artist that he'd seen in London. This trickster's main trick had been to cover himself with locked chains and then effect an escape from them. When he offered this image of himself as a poet to Frost ('I load myself with chains and try to get out of them'), the American ventured to suggest that he mustn't have too many readers, then.

For those of us who were young in the 1950s, and trying to write, the presence of Austin Clarke was a model one, an exemplary figure, a moral voice, a maker of poems out of the daily life we were all living. The appearance of *Ancient Lights* (1955), with its luminous title, was followed by that astonishing flowering of ten volumes in the late Fifties, the Sixties and the Seventies. As young students of English literature at UCD, we knew a little of Clarke from Roger McHugh, a teacher of exceptional courage in a department which was woefully conservative and hide-bound. Literature, it was suggested to us, was something that only existed in the past. Contemporary writers were a dangerous crowd, best kept outside the gates.

What was hugely stimulating to us about the Clarke poems was their immediacy, the way they spoke to us about the Ireland we were actually living in – what Clarke himself called 'the passion of real life' or 'the great ugly emotions which have shaped our national life'. In poem after poem he was demonstrating that poetry could be public and private at once, that the poet could be a witness, not only to his own, most intimate, inner journeys but also to the turning of the great, clumsy wheels of the state, pushed by the energetic, robed clerics of a triumphalist church. Above all, he demonstrated that beautiful poetry could be crafted from material that some might find ugly or distasteful. In that sense he was very much a poet for the young.

Clarke talks somewhere about the ageing Yeats and how modernism had added 'a mischievous zest to the speculation of his old age'. He might have been talking about the 'mischievous zest' of his own later poems, though in his case this came from his anger at the Ireland he had returned to before the outbreak of World War Two.

Another feature of this poetry which had us arguing into the small hours in our student flats was the questioning intelligence, the quality of mind, which informed it. This was a poetry of truth-telling, dealing with the specific, the concrete, with 'what man has made', as he puts it, but subjecting everything to an intellectual scrutiny that was thrilling to read on the page.

We had some sense, too, that the younger Irish poets, like Thomas Kinsella and John Montague and others, had turned to the older poet as a guide, and of how he gave them a very generous hearing in his little book on Irish poetry (*Poetry in Modern Ireland*). Desmond O'Grady, the youngest poet considered by Clarke in that essay was a friend of ours, although he was then living in Paris. We were also aware of the beginnings of a debate about Austin Clarke's achievement at the time and the question of how those extraordinary late poems connected to his earlier work.

In that rare book which Liam Miller brought out as a tribute to Clarke on his seventieth birthday, you had a younger Irish poet, Montague, and a younger academic critic Denis Donoghue talking about the poetry from very different perspectives. Speaking for his own generation Montague said that Clarke 'has opened up the Gaelic tradition for Irish writers in English', and that he had 'helped us to learn how to write English poetry with an Irish accent'. This is the historical importance of Austin Clarke, another transmission between one poet and another.

For Donoghue, Austin Clarke in the 1950s was 'an artist coming into his strength'. He thought, however, that the more recent work greatly over-shadowed the early work; for him there is simply no comparison between the two. When, in the early 1970s he was to write about Clarke again, he made a relatively limited list of later poems which he called 'superb'.

I think Denis was put off by the local emphasis in Clarke, particularly in the long poems, and by the persistent note of complaint in the writing. I also think he disliked the anti-clericalism, although if he and Clarke had known then what we know now about clerical behaviour, things might have been different for both of them.

I believe the publication of this volume will challenge Denis Donoghue's view and endorse Montague's. From the very beginning there is that remarkable technique. Clarke was a master craftsman of the poetic line from early on. There is also a very real substantial achievement in Clarke's early long poems in which he brings to life a buried Gaelic world for English-speaking readers. And everywhere in the early volumes you meet that exquisite lyricism with that characteristic, cold, metallic ring of Clarke, the pealing of truth behind the image, as in these lines from his version of Sweeney ('The Frenzy of Suibhne') written in the 1920s:

If I sleep now, the hag
Of the haggard, will steal
My feathers though I drowned her
In the dark pool of Achill
That has no sound.

When tides were baying
The moon, in a glen
Of pools, I fed on
Grey cowdung: a hundred
Men hauling a slab
Upon the great dolmen
Of Sweeny the King,
From the shovels and barrow,

Fled. Nailing, I dug up
The gold cup and collar
And hid them in rain.
But how can mind hurry
As reeds without feet,
And why is there pain in
A mind that is dead?

In our student days we associated Austin Clarke with a group of writers born in the twentieth century into an Ireland which was moving into independence. These writers were of Catholic background, educated, sophisticated, highly intelligent, having a direct knowledge of both Gaelic and European traditions. We would have included Mervyn Wall and Flann O'Brien in this list. Both of them, too, were presences in the Dublin of the 1950s and we loved their work because it was disruptive, suggesting a kind of freedom which, perhaps, we didn't enjoy ourselves. These writers, along with Clarke, were exploding some of the deceiving myths of the country. They were looking to a future in the way they dissected the present and the past. Their vision, like Clarke's, was essentially comic but with icy depths below the comedy. They viewed their new state with a mocking, ironic, satirical view.

They looked back to Joyce, not Yeats, and that dark papish line in Irish writing, back to George Moore and William Carleton. Clarke met Yeats, Joyce and Moore. There is fellow feeling in his encounters with the latter two that is never there in his encounters with Yeats. And there is the shared amusement as when Joyce, in Paris, sighing and silenced by his secret burdens, suddenly breaks off and asks the young Clarke: 'Is Mulvanney's shop still there at the corner?'

Sometimes it is suggested that Austin Clarke stands in isolation. I don't see it that way at all. I see him as part of a fellowship which represents some of the most significant Irish writing of the last century.

Austin Clarke: Collected Poems (Carcanet Press / The Bridge Press, 2008), edited by R Dardis Clarke, priced €23.95.

Conor O'Callaghan

THIS FAR SOUTH

We whoop lots and swap firsthand stick-up yarns.
We worship the Lamb of God on medium wave,
shoot eight-ball in pubs the size of jumbo hangars.

Here, fireworks get flogged off the hard shoulder,
a goods loco drags its solitary organ note downtown,
the Queen's shilling is accepted at stratospheric rates.

We sport Stetsons with our Celtic jerseys.
We roll our own Virginia shag, brew ale pale,
can't rightly recollect where certain skeletons are laid.

The nearest nine-holes is a future interstate corridor,
the price of gasoline a terror. A Free Presbyterian
in this neck of the parish goes by Duane McConkey.

We sign on in the six counties, say grace before grits,
bricklay new developments about the airport,
cross the channel one home fixture in every month.

Sundays spin beyond their ken to Hillsville, Ardglass.
Wagon wheels decorate the outsides of roadhouses.
The same numbers do two types of lottery docket.

We smoke turkey drumsticks at hurdy-gurdy fairs,
pack our Dodge Durangos with knock-off snooker balls
and give unmarked customs cars the runaround.

A decent skin next door was big shakes in the Klan.
The ditches these parts are fertilized with totalled Fords,
horizons late June striped by marching season flares.

We steer a middling course between *cratur* and *critter*,
inhabit ranch prefabs on the outer edges of nowhere,
sing dumb, *sir* and *ma'am* with the best of them,

bury rods on someone else's land, drown kitten litters,
trawl rivers clean of white trout, soup up jalopies,
talk bullocks, believe yodelling to be a class of trad.

This far south the drawl isn't rare or drawn enough
to either pole to be so handily placed or taken off,
the kinship insufficiently thick to slice and butter.

We hear a rattlesnake rattling in the yard after dark
as a horsebox being backed across our cattlegrid.
We hear it being backed up to the gable and no further.

Conor O'Callaghan

AMONG OTHER THINGS

The rest
have driven to the mall.
Any second now
it'll be too dark.

This close to the edge,
among other things,
I read.

Leaves rattle overhead.
Little pockets
of canned applause
sift through
the screened porch
in next door's yard.

Jesse P Ferguson

PILLOW TALK

In sleep's unguarded, open-mouthed moments,
they say, the average person
will unwittingly swallow 8 spiders per annum.
Waif bodies seeking that final dark nook,
finding instead dissolution
in the stomach's chyme corner.
Life feeds you bits of death
to build your resistance.

But all metaphoricity aside, that's 64 legs
creeping down the hatch,
some maybe as wisp-thin as the tiny blond hairs
on your cheek and chin, which I can't quite see
in the blue-grey half light that penetrates
our drapes (but I know they're there).

Our sleeping bodies, it seems,
are more hospitable than our waking selves
would like to know or admit.

Making a mental note to check
the bedding before tomorrow night,
I contemplate closing your slack,
somewhat pouty lips, perhaps cutting back
your intake of the crawling
chips-off-the-darkness-block from 8 to 7.
I think of this, backing myself into the corner
of thought's hermetic box,
then, rolling over, think better of it.

David Kennedy

CÉZANNE AT LES TROIS SAUTETS

The vault
    of large trees
        over the water.
    The vault

of large trees
    deep in the water.
        What we see
    is what we see

decomposing
    into what we see,
        like naked flesh
    entering water

in the open air
    or pre-dawn clouds
        evaporating
    as the sun hits

our eyeballs
    and our humming brain
        is skewered
    and sliced

by birdsong.
    The day rolls out
        and long before
    noon yawns,

song and brain
    blunt each other
        and nothing remains
    but a paradox:

'the manifold picture
      of nature', still
            there, and there,
      and there, the breathless,

smarting challenges
      of its suffering
            and pleasure.
      On the banks

of the Arc, he wrote,
      'I could occupy
            myself for months
      without changing place'.

The vault
      of large trees
            over the water,
      ringing with reds

and yellows,
      over the water,
            waiting to be set off
      by a touch of blue.

Les Trois Sautets: a small bridge across the River Arc, near Palette, where
Cézanne used to paint during the last months of his life.

Kit Fryatt

LOADED WITH FRUIT

Eiléan Ní Chuilleanáin, *Selected Poems* (Gallery Press, 2008), €20 hbk.
Eiléan Ní Chuilleanáin, *Selected Poems* (Faber and Faber / Gallery Press, 2008), £12.99 pbk.

It is unusual to wish a *Selected Poems* were a *Collected*; the reverse is more usual. Well-made as this selection of Eiléan Ní Chuilleanáin's poetry is, it prompts that rare desire. Her work has been selected before, for successive editions of *The Second Voyage* in 1977 and 1986. This attractively-designed book (it is worth paying a very little extra for the Gallery hardback, with its jacket illustration evocative of 'Deaths and Engines') decisively supersedes those, which were arranged without regard to the chronology of individual volumes and do not tell the reader from which collections the poems were chosen. That scattiness is redressed here, and we see clearly how assured and consistent is Ní Chuilleanáin's achievement.

The selections from her first two books are generous enough to show that confidence was present from the start: of thirty-five poems in her début *Acts and Monuments* (1972), fourteen appear here. All deserve their place; it will be possible for most readers to think of two or three others that might have joined them (my choices are 'A Midwinter Prayer' and 'The House Remembered'). Some early work is definitive of the poet's abiding concerns and tone. 'Lucina Schynning in Silence of the Nicht' ranges around her area of scholarly expertise and around the British Isles, alluding to William Dunbar's apocalyptic dream-vision in a seventeenth-century Irish or sixteenth-century English setting (an iconoclastic Cromwell has left the scene; characteristically, the poet does not specify whether it is Thomas or Oliver). 'Foreseeable Future' heralds a voice of reserved but thoroughgoing irreverence; 'Swineherd' displays controlled, harmonious wit. The latter, and 'Deaths and Engines', a lyric in the second person without a trace of the sentimentality which often accompanies that mode, remain among her best poems.

Ní Chuilleanáin has for the most part resisted the thematical turn in modern poetry, which during her career has come to seem something akin to a tyranny of the poetic 'project' – making a rational and navigable selection of her work all the more important. In an interview published in the *Irish University Review* last year, Ní Chuilleanáin speaks of her rejection of 'programmatic' poetics: 'I am not that kind of poet. I find that American poets, in particular…set out to write twenty-five poems about this or that. Mine would not be like that. I have a definite feeling that each poem will stand up on its own.' She attributes recurrent ideas and figures to her habit of revising poems in small batches, rather than to overarching design; if this is strategic modesty, it is also refreshing and rebellious. Ní Chuilleanáin has nonetheless written three sequences of some length, all of which are represented here. 'Site of Ambush' is unhappily selected to make sense of a line in 'Gloss / Clós / Glas' (a poem for which I cannot share an affection otherwise apparently unanimous), but it is good to see the best of the poems from 'Cork' once again attributed to that diffuse but appealing work, while the choice from 'The Rose Geranium' is unexceptionable.

If the architectonic is in short supply, there is no corresponding lack of architecture. Ní Chuilleanáin's poems about domestic and ecclesiastical buildings – in particular the convent interiors which combine parlour and cloister – have attracted sometimes laborious commentary, which contrives to obscure both their mischief and their grandeur. The first thing to say about 'Fireman's Lift' or 'The Architectural Metaphor', for example, is surely that they are *funny*: they seek to delight us with syntactical and fig-ural play. 'The Architectural Metaphor' is not the worse for wearing its reflexivity a little heavily, eluding the reader's question 'metaphor for what?' with an audacious bit of *grand guignol* machinery, which in turn resolves into a way back to humanity from the Gothic. 'Fireman's Lift', a subtler performance, conjures the monumental intimacy of the Assumption fresco that decorates the cupola of Parma Cathedral. Ní Chuilleanáin amasses clauses in imitation of Correggio's dense press of angelic bodies:

> This is what love sees, that angle:
> The crick in the branch loaded with fruit,
> A jaw defining itself, a shoulder yoked,
>
> The back making itself a roof
> The legs a bridge, the hands
> A crane and a cradle.

The unemphatic vowel music ('loaded…shoulder yoked') and consonantal pairs ('back' / 'making', 'itself' / 'roof') see that the alliteration 'crane' / 'cradle' clicks rather than clangs into place. Following the poem to its conclusion ('the muscles clung and shifted / For a final purchase together / Under her weight as she came to the edge of the cloud') the reader realis-es that the poem embodies not only the fresco's daft magnificence, but also our feelings about poetic enactment. Any attempt to reproduce the world in words is attended by a splendid indignity.

Such intricate self-reflexivity risks another kind of programmatism. Poetry invokes that which is not itself by drawing attention to itself; that is, to the language of which it is made. The world-conjuring which is poetry's only abiding duty is separated from trivial linguistic diversion by the slenderest of margins. The last poem of the selection, 'Gloss / Clós / Glas' strays only a very little from the task of making words rise up before us as things, and does so rather from excess than deficiency of love for language, but the effect is one of pastiche. It has every feature we might expect of Ní Chuilleanáin: a half-domestic, half-institutional setting, a scholar given the 'nightwork' of a fairytale hero, reflection upon the texture of words and objects, a startling final turn. And yet each element is minutely overstated. 'Raking the dictionaries, darting at locked presses, / Hunting for keys' savours faintly of the desperation of a movie director charged with making intellectual life visually exciting. 'Reflection' and 'gloss' solidify in a hefty figurative cluster of mirrors, polished wood, water and sleek fur. The poem's last simile takes us from the labours of folktale to a quizzical play of thought, a transition imbrued with the disappointment which accompanies literary revision of traditional material. Ní Chuilleanáin is too thoughtful a poet-scholar for that effect to be accidental, but neither its deliberateness nor her deliberation upon it is an entire solution to the problem presented by traditional and folk material in modern poetry.

We do that material itself an injury when we attribute dissatisfaction with literary versions to dilettante taste for quaint simplicity, for the existence of the discontent actually indicates a diminution of art. Coming to Coleridge after 'Sir Patrick Spens' we are not disappointed, but I can think of no reworking of anonymous traditions by a living writer that is not, in some sense, a letdown. The remedy usually suggested is that poets simply stop rummaging around in the myth-kitty: that they cease 'looking to the past' or something of the sort. More sophisticated versions of this solution instruct poets to render any application of folk tradition relevant through psychological aptness, historical parallel, or poetic structure (I sometimes suspect that the broad highway to the 'project' is paved with *poetic structure*). The cruder of these injunctions accounts for the appeal of traditional material rather better than the supposedly subtler: the attraction of folklore is not its potential to make sense of our atavisms (which in any case is very nearly nil) but the opportunity it offers to indulge them. Its uncanny impersonality is analogous to the deconstructionist notion that language, in Paul de Man's words, 'does things which are so radically out of our control that they cannot be assimilated to the human at all.' It might well be better, ethically speaking, to drown the myth-kitty than strain to accommodate it to an age of human rights.

But poetry is not made or unmade by its ethics. When we are unhappy with a modern interpretation of a myth or traditional tale, it is not the subject matter which has failed us by being either too much possessed by the past or insufficiently racy of the soil, but the poet's art. Ní Chuilleanáin's art is better than most – she is by far the best Irish poet working in this mode and among the best in English. If she nods occasionally to produce folklore boilerplate, all salt-scoured hair, snow and sloes, it serves the better to show that so many of her contemporaries spend all their time in the land of Nod. Commenting on her translations of Ileana Mălăncioiu, Ní Chuilleanáin remarks that 'Images are easier to translate than delicate verbal effects' – but her achievement, where she succeeds, is to render them indistinguishable. It is a shame that none of her translations are represented here, except 'Kilcash' and a variation on Leopardi's 'La quiete dopo la tempesta'. For a selection of her fine versions of Nuala Ní Dhomhnaill and Mălăncioiu, we must await the *Collected Poems* that this book might have been.

Paddy Bushe

TRANSLATING MERMAIDS AND MOURNING

Nuala Ní Dhomhnaill, *The Fifty Minute Mermaid*, translated by Paul
Muldoon (The Gallery Press), €13.90.
Vona Groarke, *Lament for Art O'Leary*, from the Irish of Eibhlín Dubh Ní
Chonaill (The Gallery Press), €10.

These two books make interesting shelf-fellows: two Gaelic women,
both steeped in Gaelic tradition, and at the same time both highly
individual and personal, both translated by very fine poets. Both use
traditional modes, one that of the *caoineadh*, the other that of *seanchas*,
on which to stamp their very personal creativity. The contrasts are
interesting also. Separated by more than two centuries, one, an outpouring
of grief for a murdered husband, in part communally and traditionally
expressed, was initially orally transmitted, with a consequent fluidity as
to text and even to authorship, and it waited many years for its now
multiple translations; the other is an intensely literary and individual use
of a virtually dead oral tradition in order to, among many other things,
explore the communal loss and trauma implied by that death, as well as
exploring the trauma its author has undergone in her own life. As might
be expected in the case of a contemporary writer of such stature, translation took place much sooner, although not in the simultaneous way which
is becoming questionably more common in Ireland. Both books, as
might be expected from Gallery Press, are handsomely produced, the
cover of *Lament for Art O'Leary* being particularly well-chosen and
designed.
        This collection of Nuala Ní Dhomhnaill, translated by Paul Muldoon,
has been enthusiastically reviewed at home and abroad. No surprise
there; both poets deserve the accolades. This is poetry and poetry
translation of the highest calibre. What is surprising is how many people
have taken it for granted that this is new work by Ní Dhomhnaill. It is a
measure of the task faced by Irish language poetry in gaining recognition
to realise that the original publication of these poems in book form
happened in the last century. *Cead Aighnis* (An Sagart, 1998), a considerably
larger collection than that under review, was very favourably reviewed by
Deirdre Brennan in *PIR* 63. Yet, and perhaps this is inevitable even in
Ireland, poems in Irish seem to make their real début when they are
translated. Luckily for the integrity of poetry and of publishing in Irish,
Ní Dhomhnaill insists that her initial publication be monolingual. Gallery
Press does have an acknowledgement of the initial publication, but

rather discreetly tucked away at the back. And the acknowledgement is for 'poems by Nuala Ní Dhomhnaill which were first published in…', which would suggest just a few poems, rather than, as is the case, all of the new book except for three poems. I think the acknowledgement, out of respect for the original publication, as well as for the cultural commitment involved in monolingual publication, could have been more generous.

I have sometimes been exasperated by the exuberance, to put it one way, of Muldoon's previous translations of Ní Dhomhnaill. But when Muldoon is good, he is very, very good. And here he is almost always very good. His versions of the three poems which make up the first section of the book, perhaps in deference to their deep and dark seriousness, are both authoritative and responsive and, above all, and although it may sound prissy, they are respectful. And – something which is hugely important for an Irish readership – they can send the uncertain reader of the original back to that original with an understanding and appreciation of it. At the same time, they can stand as poems in their own right. What more can be asked for?

As an example of wonderful poetry wonderfully translated, I would like to take a closer look at one of these, the poem 'Dubh', and Muldoon's version, 'Black'. It is one of Ní Dhomhnaill's finest poems, written in the immediate aftermath of the Srebrenica massacre in 1995. The insistent, intrusive drumbeat of 'dubh', combined with a litany of the everyday and the internal blacknesses through which the poet apprehends the day, make for a powerfully oppressive poem:

> Mar táimse dubh.
> Tá mo chroí dubh
> is m'intinn dubh.
> Tá m'amharc ar feadh raon mo radhairc dubh.
> Tá an dubh istigh is amuigh agam chughainn.

Muldoon carries this into English with style and with loyalty. Most of his translation, as is appropriate for the awful simplicity of the original, is simple and literal, but it carries the ominous rhythm and heavy vowels of the original, and is never awkward:

> The ox is black.
> The hound is black.
> The very horse from Iveragh is black.

But when Muldoon has to depart from the original, for idiomatic or semantic reasons, he does so with flair and insight. Ní Dhomhnaill's 'gach dubh ina gheal' of political reaction becomes 'persuade us / to look on the bright side', the Irish 'an dubh a chur ina gheal ort' not being available in English. The idiomatic 'Tá an dubh istigh is amuigh agam chughainn', which is not literally translatable, becomes 'There's a black mark against all our names', which keeps the sense of communal hatred and guilt, also adding the chilling echo of lists and purges. The same politicians who in Irish are 'ar sciobaidh' are 'scuffling about' in English to explain things. That device of the phonic echo to complement or replace an exact correspondence of meaning is used again when a bird 'a scinneann amach as an ealta' becomes 'suddenly out of sync with the flock'. And the final word, literally, shows Muldoon's mastery. After the dark litany of the poem, after the overpowering repetition of 'dubh', Ní Dhomhnaill tells us that Srebrenica, 'cathair an airgid', is now 'bán'. The sense of this ending depends on the ambiguity that 'bán', as well as white, means empty, or devastated. Quite a challenge for the translator. Muldoon's quite brilliant 'blank' not only adequately translates the meaning, but also makes a phonic and visual link with 'black' that is an adequate replacement for the link of contraries in the original. It also carries the echo of 'my mind is blank' which is so inherent in the poem. It is a superb ending to a superb translation of a superb poem.

The other two poems in this opening section, again poems of the first rank, are equally well-served: 'an file iomráiteach Seirbeach / a bhí ina cheannaire ar mhórchampa géibhinn' cleverly and validly becomes 'the major Serbian poet / who was the commandant of a major camp' in 'An Obair' / 'The Task', a poem in which the title is a play on the Irish name for Nobber in Co Meath, a task Muldoon accomplishes easily. But his exuberance breaks out now and again as when in 'Mo Mháistir Dorcha' / 'My Dark Master' the line 'Luíonn siad síos i móineir' must have been deemed botanically challenged, because it transforms itself into 'They lie down in pastures of clover and fescue / and lucerne.'

In *Cead Aighnis*, the poems which make up the second part of this collection were collectively known as 'Na Murúcha a Thriomaigh'. While the title under review, which apparently refers to the length of a psychiatrist's consultation, is clever, it seems to me that it limits the collection to one of its aspects. So does Muldoon's translation of the name of what had been the original title poem: 'The Assimilated Merfolk', a title that is subverted by the poem itself. What would be wrong with the neutral 'The Merfolk on Dry Land', for example? I dwell on this only because it seems to me that to label this collection solely in terms of personal psychological trauma, or race-memory, or its loss, or the losses and gains of cultural change and assimilation, or folkloric exploration, or social satire or whatever, as has sometimes been done since its publication, is to do it less than justice. It partakes of all of these things, but it is vitally and energetically far, far more, and it should not be confined.

'Cuimhne an Uisce' / 'A Recovered Memory of Water' is a case in point.
It is deeply serious and comical, vividly concrete and domestic, and
wrestles with personal and communal loss, alienation, and therapeutic
attempts towards recovery, as well as the process of writing itself, all in
less than forty lines. All of this thematic weight, however, is secondary to
the poetry of lines like:

> 'Slaod tanaí,' a thugann sí air,
> í ag tóraíocht go cúramach i measc na bhfocal.
> 'Brat gléineach, ábhar silteach, rud fliuch.'

> 'A thin flow', she calls it,
> casting about gingerly in the midst of words.
> 'A shiny film. Dripping stuff. Something wet.'

This richness of image and rhythm creates in this collection an extraordinary atmosphere, literally full of wonders. The dreamlike fluidity
between the various worlds involved allows many explorations, personal,
cultural, linguistic, political and many more, without the necessity for
consistency or rationality that a more conventional approach might
demand. The world of the merfolk can suggest the perceived rich romantic
communality of a lost Gaelic world, as in the conventional image of the
Blasket world; it can also be stupid, vicious and intolerant. It allows Ní
Dhomhnaill to give us a multifaceted glimpse into worlds which can
reflect cultural dilemmas and aspects of her own troubled psyche at the
same time, without the need to tidy up the contradictions and confusions
that this necessarily involves. And lest we idealise any lost worlds and
their cultures, the last poem in the book, 'Spléachanna Fánacha ar an
dTír-fó-Thoinn' / 'Some Observations on Land-Under-Wave', leaves us,
having negotiated an entrance through some heroically romantic place
like the Giant's Causeway or Fingal's cave, with a list of what we might
find among its empty rooms. And the list reads like an inventory from a
Nazi death-camp: gold teeth, earrings, eyeglasses, garment-piles, and 'go
háirithe mórán Éireann drochghallúnach' / 'including a mountain of low-
grade soap.' However, I prefer to leave this marvellous book with these
lines:

> Tá dearmhad glan déanta acu
> faoin am seo ar shuathadh mearathail na gcaisí doimhne
> is ar chlaisceadal na míol mór sa duibheagán.

> By now they've clean forgotten
> the dizzying churning of the deep currents
> and, from the abyss, the whales' antiphonal singing.
>   – 'NA MURÚCHA A THRIOMAIGH' / 'THE ASSIMILATED MERFOLK'

Vona Groarke's new translation of the *Lament for Art O'Leary* takes as its starting point a wish to have a version 'that tried to nail how much Eileen really *fancied* her husband', as she tells us in her introduction. It is an ambition that leads to some wonderful things. For example, her final stanza:

> Rise up now and come with me,
> for the weight of sorrow
> across my heart
> will not lift
> unless you pitch it off.
> It is like a chest
> with stones in it
> and I am very much afraid
> that its rusted lock
> and fastened latch
> will never know a key.

This is a valid and vivid version of the traditional motif that Eibhlín Dubh uses (I quote from Seán Ó Tuama's edition of the poem, published by An Clócomhar, 1961):

> Ní scaipfidh ar mo chumha
> Atá i lár mo chroí á bhrú,
> Dúnta suas go dlúth
> Mar a bheadh glas a bheadh ar thrúnc
> 'S go raghadh an eochair amú.

Groarke has foregrounded the sexual basis of the image, and made a lovely word-play between the English meanings of 'chest'. She has also chosen to end the poem with this stanza, rather than with the stanza Ó Tuama used to end his edition. This is a valid editorial decision if we go by Ó Tuama's notes on the manuscript material, and a very strong ending, especially given Groarke's declared translatory emphasis. This is translation which is genuinely illuminating, as well as poetry in itself. So is:

> I thought, when I bought
> that suit for you, it would slip
> between you and all harm...

for

Óir do shíleas féinig
Ná maródh an saol thú
Nuair a cheannaíos duit éide...

And Groarke uses rhyme beautifully to translate

Nuair a lamhadh an piléar leat
Go ngeobhainn é im thaobh dheas
Nó i mbinn mo léine...

as

I could have smothered it
in the folds of my dress
or the folds of my breasts...

But there are places where the translation falls down. Sometimes it's just inaccuracies that seem to have no rationale:

To my shame, I smirked
at the big talk
that I'd heard from you so often.

is a distortion of Eibhlín Dubh's 'Níor dheineas ded chaint ach magadh' in response to her husband's premonition of danger. And

I plunged my two fists
in your spilled blood
and sucked from my useless fingers.

seems to me to be absolutely inadequate for and distortive of the ritual grief of

Do chuid fola leat 'na sraithibh
is níor fhanas le hí ghlanadh
Ach í ól suas lem basaibh.

And this brings me to what I see as a major problem with this translation. Those last three lines of the original depend enormously, as does the entire poem, on the insistent battering of rhyme. Breandán Ó Buachalla has pointed out that rhyme is a defining characteristic of the poem. So is the 'beaten out in line after three-stressed line' rhythm that Seamus Heaney refers to. Groarke adverts to Heaney's observation in her introduction, but says she had to dispense with the rhythm to avoid monotony and staleness. A fair point of view, although by no means unarguable with. But she doesn't refer at all to the loss of rhyme. She is very aware of the 'the music of its art' in the original, and of its 'highwire tension' between this music and the 'unrelenting steady nerve of it, and the extremes of passion contained therein'. At times, she says, she added image or metaphor to give an inkling of this. But, as Seán Ó Tuama has pointed out, the poem depends on its dramatic force, rather than imagistic or metaphoric intensity. It seems to me that rhythm and rhyme are an intrinsic part of the meaning of Caoineadh Airt Uí Laoghaire, and that, if they cannot be mirrored to a significant extent, that some equivalent pattern of sound would have to be found for translation. A version which would simply take the poem as its starting point, and which could stretch itself thereafter in many directions, might indeed be a very worthwhile experiment. I think Vona Groarke might do a brilliant job of such a project.

But while this translation has lovely things in it, and certainly illuminates some aspects of the poem, it seems to me to have fallen between two stools. In the meantime, I think that Eilís Dillon's translation, which, *pace* the introduction to this book, is not a shortened version of the poem, remains the best way for English speakers into the original.

Tom Hubbard

MOVING UPON SILENCE

Enda Coyle-Greene, *Snow Negatives* (Dedalus Press, 2007), €11.
Fred Johnston, *The Oracle Room* (Cinnamon Press, 2007), £7.99.
Mark Roper, *Even So: New and Selected Poems* (Dedalus Press, 2008), €14.

Here are three seminars on how to be mellow without being cosy. The poets were all born in the early 1950s. Fred Johnston's lament for Beatle George Harrison is also a lament for lost youth, richly suggestive of images and sounds that aren't actually in the poem's text – bell-bottomed trousers and Liverpudlian accents filling out his inscribed arena of 'girls shy-legging it', lank hair and all manner of late 1960s/70s accoutrements which we just assumed would always be with us. 'The flash-Harry wee lads now fat and fifty, / Swinging on your every word.'

Coyle-Greene's very title *Snow Negatives* – surely a poem in itself – sets the tone for much in these collections. You don't necessarily have to be of the poets' (and my) generation to go with this. Let's say you're under c. 40 and still possess an unreconstructed (great-)grandparent or you otherwise love hanging out in junk shops: then you, too, will feel a shock of recognition at Coyle-Greene's references, in 'Radio Geography', to the old stations of Athlone and Hilversum that were displayed on the wireless as one (i.e. we oldies) twiddled knobs to position the dial right where one wanted it. Nostalgia? Yes, and why not. Today's current thirty-somethings, or the more alert among them, will recognise their own equivalents of what is past, and passing, and to come. I found Mark Roper's book full of eerie echoes, intentionally or otherwise: take this, the opening of his 'Goldcrest':

> Fair enough its thin pheet-pheet in a conifer;
> fair enough a glimpse of yellow crest.
> But this one flew straight into this glass door
> and dropped on this metal balcony at my feet...

I couldn't get out of my mind the Venerable Bede's celebrated image of the bird which flies into the hall then out of it: image, that is, of transience. I infer that Roper, like Bede, has a background as a Geordie, so maybe that shared geocultural space has something to do with it. In Roper's poem, though, the bird's flight is interrupted, violently, before it unexpectedly recovers and flies off again. Twenty-first century equivalent? Roper is no-nonsense, anti-anthropomorphic about it. The bird 'Got on / with its business. So I got on with mine.'

These collections owe much of their strength to what is unspoken and implied: significant absences and silences. Roper offers the tribute of poetry to that most eloquently mute of arts, painting, in 'Manet's "The Fifer"' and 'Van Gogh's "The Farm"'. I wouldn't downplay these poets' responses to nature, but my own view is that there is greater resonance in responses to culture. Poet as subtlest form of art critic? That was the possibility held out (and vindicated) by the likes of Baudelaire and Rilke. It seemed fitting that, more than half-way through Roper's volume, I encountered 'Palm: *after Rilke*'. Rilkean tropes – even on one occasion an echo ('You must learn how to love') rather than an actual translation of a certain line ('Du mußt dein Leben ändern') – animate this book. 'Palm' is in fact a superb summing-up, in English, of the preoccupations of that great pan-European poet. 'Inner shell shaped / to a fruit formed in prayer': Rilke, friend and interpreter of Rodin, understood the calmly powerful gestures of the human hand. 'Broken home of wholeness': there we have that terrifying antithesis, omnipresent in *The Notebooks of Malte Laurids Brigge*, pertaining to a Europe just a few years away from war. Roper's Co Kilkenny expands beyond his time and its space. Not dissimilarly, Coyle-Greene deploys a late photograph of F Scott Fitzgerald:

> so that later, in the studio,
> there was nothing left of him, no trace
> of his stare to be sieved through hard glass
> by the aspic glare of the camera's
> hooded, sudden eye.
>   – 'EARLIER THAT DAY'

With such a range of cultural reference, the melancholic vibes of these books can't be dismissed as posy self-indulgence.

Yet – and this is where Fred Johnston draws us up – certain silences are far from benign. Good anger requires a voice to be clearly heard, though even here it's the subdued tone that works, more effectively surely than any decibelled rant (however justified that might be). Johnston rages measuredly and devastatingly against an Ireland whose windows were not so much squinting as boarded-up, where child abusers in high places were allowed to flourish while would-be whistle-blowers were at best ignored and at worst threatened. Moreover, it's not all past tense nor for that matter is it limited to home-grown malevolences:

> Now that the poetry's over
> There's Gaza and Iraq,
> And the crooked politicians
> Doing deals behind our back.

[…]

The Yanks still dump their soldiers
In our airports and hotels:
No poet worth a travel-grant
Dare sound the warning bells.

       – 'LINES WRITTEN AFTER A POETRY FESTIVAL'

That's a street poetry looking for a street. Fred Johnston demonstrates that, in 2008/09, it's not passé to be *engagé*.

Nessa O'Mahony

WOMEN FOR ALL SEASONS

Catherine Phil MacCarthy, *Suntrap* (Blackstaff Press, 2007), £7.99.
Joan Newmann, Kate Newmann, *Belongings* (Arlen House, 2007), €15.
Nuala Ní Chonchúir, *Tattoo : Tatú* (Arlen House, 2007), €15.

Impossible not to be drawn, on a dreary November afternoon, by the prisms of light refracting from the work of these four writers.

There is illumination aplenty in *Suntrap*, Catherine Phil MacCarthy's third collection. In the title poem, a young child is initiated into knowledge when she is shown, for the first time, how a magnifying glass works with light; the resulting epiphany – ' … my palm under it / is pink, fantastic' and the poem's concluding line, 'I learn for the first time how to burn' – capture the perfect duality of innocence and experience that is a recurring theme in this fine collection. The penultimate poem, 'Inheritance', once again uses sunlight to explore transience; the 'old house / abandoned now / looks in on itself' where once its 'deep windows…catch the sun'.

These are poems of contrasts: youth and age, light and dark, the wild and the tame. MacCarthy seems constantly aware of the feral layer that lies beneath the skin. In 'The Freedom of the City', the 'old man with keys in his hand' spotted escorting a young women with 'pouting lips / and long ethnic skirts' brings to mind, with his cautious surveying of the territory, a 'bushy-tailed / red fox whose eyes met mine / in our garden after rain'. In 'Gráinne's Bed', the lover (Diarmuid, one guesses) is so at one with the natural world he seems almost a part of it:

> On this grassy mound, my love,
> you are meshed in a web of blossom,
> pale body entwined with stems,
>
> violets, heartsease, wild roses.

But the natural world is not always so benign, as poems such as 'Sparrow Thieves' and 'Terriers' warn.

Reading these poems, it strikes me that MacCarthy is a Romantic poet in the original sense; for her, landscape and nature provide a nurse to the imagination and the soul. She paints that landscape with exquisite skill; hers is a quiet, steady, understated and always pleasurable type of poetry.

Mother and daughter Joan and Kate Newmann have themselves acted many's a time as nurse to the imagination and soul of many a nascent poet through their good work at Summer Palace Press, so it is good news that Arlen House has chosen to foreground their own significant talents in this joint publication. *Belongings* includes some 68 of Joan's poems and 63 of Kate's, many of which have previously appeared in journals (such as this one) and anthologies. Though there is no apparent thematic link, other than the notion of where the poet belongs in her world, it is tempting to read the collection as a dialogue, if not between self and soul, then between the 'home' and 'away' sides of their two personalities. Joan's poems are very much of 'home', raiding memory and often offering chatty, beautifully detailed reminiscences that are grounded with local references; for example in 'Passing the Sign to Drumbanagher and the Dromantine Missions' we get this captivating opening:

> It was the day we went on the bus fifty-two years ago
> and Muriel told me about the woman
> who had been stung by a bee
> and the bee was still a lump above her eye...

There is a sense here of being in the company of a supreme story teller, whiling away the hours with tales and cups of tea. The constant use of first names – the same Muriel appears in a number of poems while Lily and Kathleen make regular appearances – heightens this sense of the cosily domestic, yet one comes away from the poems with the notion of having learned something larger about the world. Perhaps Joan Newmann wants us to see how connected we all are with each other; that in a society that increasingly emphasises divisiveness and individualism, we can still learn from an older, more innocent age.

Kate Newmann's poems range more widely; instead of the dances at Port-na-Blagh described by her mother we are brought to the house of Christopher Columbus, to the vineyards of Chile, to Neruda's house on the Isla Negra (not to mention his homes at Valparaiso and Santiago). But these aren't mere travelogues; the first poems remind us of the cataclysmic impact that Columbus's journeys had on the native populations of the countries he 'discovered'; in 'What Columbus Saw' we are told he 'Saw no one until he had to see / Taino Indians taught in the language of their blood'.

The complicity that the self-aware modern traveller must acknowledge follows Newmann throughout her travels. In 'White Crosses', the 'random markers of the rotting / embrace between flesh and soil' remind her of the 'ghosts of misery, ankle-high', while in 'Zoo' a plethora of animals are seen to suffer for the amusement of tourists:

> These iguanas in a tin nightmare,
> heat pounding on metal,
> pounding on reptilian skin.
> All mistreated membrane.

There are some wonderful tableaux in this collection; Newmann wanders through Parisian streets, capturing the sights and smells, the vivid colours with an always original eye. Here is her opening to the poem 'Sacré Coeur': 'The full moon a huge flatbread / mopping up the spiced Montmartre dark.' This is also a perfect image for the great sepulchre itself, perched like a great white ball of dough on a Parisian hill.

Newmann's travels through Chile inevitably conjure up that country's most famous poet; there are several poems devoted to Neruda and the places he lived. Through them we see another side of the poet, one that displayed a passion for Russian dolls and ships in bottles, whose childhood 'colossal painted horse' reminds us of the ultimate loneliness of his old age:

> The once unattainable horse surrounded with real hay
> in the house loud with childlessness
> which only knew him old...
>   – 'THE HORSE PARLOUR'

There is compassion here, now awe; Kate Newmann's poems attest to her love of travel, but they also show her desire to tread lightly on the earth.

Bilingual poet Nuala Ní Chonchúir makes her debut with *Tatoo : Tatú* and an impressive debut it is too. In a short introductory essay, written in both Irish and English, she explains her decision to write in both languages and is critical of what she terms the elitist 'posturing' carried out in the name of Irish language preservation, arguing for a more tolerant, open and supportive approach to all those who wish to speak the native tongue. She describes the poems as 'versions' of each other rather than literal translations and points to the 'concision and beauty' in Irish that is unavailable in English.

As someone whose Irish would definitely fall foul of the purists, I am perhaps not the best judge of the extent to which the Irish and English poems do justice to each other. I can, however, find much to praise in the linguistic toughness of the English versions and the complete lack of coyness with which she writes of sexual politics. There is a witty awareness at work in poems such as 'Standing Male Nude' which is short enough to be given in full:

If the sculptor
had you recline,
supine like a woman,
all your hummocks and
hollows smoothed out,
made horizontal,
would you be unmanned?

Like many who translate, Ní Chonchúir is painfully aware of the
tensions between the translator and the original poet. In her version, in
the poem 'A Kind of Forgery', the translator acts as a type of taxidermist,
winnowing out the secrets before 'hanging a new flesh / on older bones';
the discomfort apparent here may explain why only half or so of the
poems in this collection have Irish versions. But there are many fine
poems that reveal a modern, irreverent sensibility; I was particularly
taken with her vision of Dublin (we share a home town) where:

The Liffey swills
right through you
rushing on to
empty her bladder
on the Muglin Rocks
        — DUBLINIA

Ní Chonchúir has already accrued a number of awards and distinctions
in her short career and displays a formidable energy in all her
endeavours. Certainly, her poetry, unlike her Anna Liffey, leaves the reader thirsty for more.

David Cooke

SENSING A DIFFERENCE

Colette Bryce, *Self-Portrait in the Dark* (Picador Poetry, 2008), £8.99.

Colette Bryce was born in Derry in 1970 and grew up there during the darkest years of the Troubles, although she has lived elsewhere since the age of eighteen. From the outset of her poetic career she has enjoyed conspicuous success. Her first collection, *The Heel of Bernadette*, was awarded the Aldeburgh Poetry Festival Prize for Best First Collection. She won the UK National Poetry Competition in 2003 with her poem, 'The Full Indian Rope Trick', which subsequently became the title poem for her second collection and, more impressively, won a reader's poll in 2008 as the most popular winning poem in the thirty years of that competition's existence.

Self-Portrait in the Dark is her third collection and like its predecessors it is lyrical and technically adroit. However, whilst building upon the strengths of her earlier work, it shows the poet developing an increasingly oblique, metaphysical vision of the world. There is less emphasis here on the poet's childhood and the 'spoiled inheritance' of her Northern Irish background, although it is handled movingly in 'The Harm', a sestina in which a young girl, obsessed with the idea that a ticking lamppost contains a bomb, encounters a women who rants at her for loitering on the dangerous corner where her own daughter was run over. At the end of the poem the girl has not shaken off her own obsession but has gained a new insight into another's pain:

> You are sure, as sure as the ticking
> lamppost is a bomb, its timer on, of harm, printed
> forever on the corner where the woman's world has stopped.

By way of contrast, the first poem in the collection, 'A Spider', shows Bryce at her most astringent and is an object lesson in how maximum results can be achieved by minimum means. The poem, which has only thirteen short lines, is about trapping a spider under a wine glass. The opening is worthy of Emily Dickinson:

> I trapped a spider in a glass,
> a fine-blown wineglass.
> It shut around him, silently.

The hapless creature is then described with a scientific precision reminiscent of Miroslav Holub:

> He stood still, a small wheel
> of intricate suspension, cap
> at the hub of his eight spokes,
> inked eyes on stalks; alert,
> sensing a difference.

And it is at this point that a shift occurs which takes us beyond the empirical:

> I meant to let him go
> but still he taps against the glass
> all Marcel Marceau
> in *the wall that is there and not there,*
> a circumstance I know.

In 'Car Wash' she again plays with this sense of everyday reality being briefly suspended, but to completely different effect. In this poem two women drive into what is at first seen as a masculine world, where 'This business of driving / reminds us of our fathers.' However, within the sealed-off world of an everyday utility there is a sudden change in perspective as the women are 'delighted by a wholly / unexpected privacy / of soap suds pouring, no, / *cascading* in velvety waves'. They now find that they have a new freedom which gives them the courage to 'engage in a kiss'. At the end of the poem the possibility of a new relationship is literally given the green light.

As a collection *Self-Portrait in the Dark* has an impressive coherence. As good as the individual poems frequently are, the whole adds up to more than the sum of its parts. The title poem with its suggestion of brooding introspection brings together the main themes of the book: isolation, loneliness and the fragility of human relationships. In this poem the protagonist is sitting at a window in the small hours, smoking a cigarette, two months after her lover has moved on. Dangerous territory, but what saves the poem from teetering over the edge into self-pity or sentimentality is above all its formal elegance and the precision of its language: four substantial stanzas written in the loosely rhymed irregular couplets so often favoured by Paul Muldoon:

> Beyond the daffodils
> on Magdalen Green, there's one slow vehicle
> pushing its beam along Riverside Drive,

a sign of life;
and two months on
from 'moving on'
your car, that you haven't yet picked up,
waits, spattered in raindrops like bubble wrap.

It has all the wry humour of Muldoon at his best, but avoids the whimsy
and excessive cleverness which sometimes vitiate his work:

And you don't need to know that
I've been driving it illegally at night
in the lamp-lit silence of this city
– you'd only worry –
or, worse, that Morrissey
is jammed in the tape deck now and for eternity...

There are other fine poems such as 'Finisterre', 'Nature Walk', and 'One
Night in the Glasgow Central Hotel', which examine the theme of loneliness with equal success. Mention must also be made of one astonishing
poem on this theme entitled 'Vertical Blinds'. It is spread across two
pages in four narrow strips to represent the blinds of the title. Normally
'concrete poetry' is a genre for which, I must confess, I have very little
regard. Here, however, the visual effect is allied to a remorseless,
mechanical rhythm for which the only comparison I can think of is
Beckett's minimalist prose.

Although Bryce's handling of these themes is moving, she is too
intelligent a writer not to have worked out that there are dangers inherent in excessive introspection and this is acknowledged in another prize
winning poem, 'Self-Portrait in a Broken Wing-Mirror'. Its seven ample
stanzas, written in traditional iambics, show her in complete control of
her material as she meditates upon her own face. At first she sees herself
as 'Selkirk, washed up on a beach, / in prone position surveying the
sweep / of his future sanctuary, or prison.' However, by the end she
realises that it is time to move on:

Presently, I will attempt to move,
attempt to arise in a shower of diamonds,
but first I must finish this childish contest
where one must stare the other out, not look
away, like a painting in a gallery, where
only the blink of an eye might restart time.

And throughout the collection there are poems where, as in 'Car Wash',
the possibility of new beginnings is balanced against meditations on

'aloneness'. 'The Knack' is another ruthlessly pared-down parable about picking up the pieces and getting on with your life. In 'Espresso', the poem which brings the collection to a close, it is as if the medieval lyric has been catapulted into the twenty-first century. It is Spring and the nest painstakingly constructed by a bird is compared to a small cup held by a woman as she waits in expectation of a possible new relationship. A stoic determination to make the most of life is also the theme of 'Next Year's Luck' where against the odds the protagonist is determined to look to the future.

Colette Bryce is a poet who is both scrupulous and inventive, and who, like Pasternak, is always striving to 'get to the very essence of things'. Occasionally, there is the odd poem – 'The Hunted', or 'On Highgate Hill' – which doesn't quite come together, but by and large Bryce's poetry aims at, and frequently achieves, an effortless universality.

Liam Carson

PLUNGING INTO POETRY

Elaine Feinstein, *The Russian Jerusalem: A Novel* (Carcanet Press, 2008), £9.95.
Marina Tsvetaeva, *Paths of the Beggar Woman: The Selected Poems of Marina
Tsvetaeva,* translated by Belinda Cooke (Worple Press, 2008), £12.

'I am also captivated by the fact...that there are many, many paths – just
as there are many different people and many different passions!'; so
Marina Tsvetaeva is quoted by Belinda Cooke in her introduction to *Paths
of the Beggar Woman: The Selected Poems of Marina Tsvetaeva*. The title
alludes, of course, to Tsvetaeva's tragic and peripatetic life. She spent years
in exile from Soviet Russia in Prague and in Paris. When her husband
Sergei Efron – a former White Russian soldier – was exposed as a Soviet
spy, she and her family returned to their native land. There they became
victims of Stalin's Terror. Efron was executed; her daughter Alya sent to
the Gulag. Tsvetaeva herself was shunned by former friends. As Hitler's
armies advanced, she fled with her son Mur to Elabuga in the Tatar
Republic. Reduced to total penury – she could not even get a job as a
washerwoman – she slipped further and further into depression, and
hanged herself in 1941.

For Simon Karlinsky, Tsvetaeva's story crystallises the horrors of
Stalin's era: 'Exile, neglect, persecution and suicide may have been the fate
of Russian poets after the Revolution, but perhaps only Marina Tsvetaeva
experienced *all* these'. Exile and wandering is the historical experience of
the Jewish people, and is a theme in Tsvetaeva's 'Poem of the End'*:

> Wouldn't it be a hundred times better
> To become the Wandering Jew?
> For anyone not scum,
> Life is a pogrom.
> — TRANSLATED BY NINA KOSSMAN

> Ghetto of the chosen. Beyond this
>   ditch. No mercy
> In this   most Christian of worlds
>   all poets   are Jews.
> — TRANSLATED BY ELAINE FEINSTEIN

---

*The Kossmann quote is from *Poem of the End: Selected Narrative and Lyrical Poems* by
Marina Tsvetaeva (Ardis, 2004); all Feinstein quotes are from the revised edition of *Marina
Tsvetaeva: Selected Poems* (Carcanet, 1999).

Elaine Feinstein's *The Russian Jerusalem: A Novel*, is an exquisite blend of memoir, poetry, history, reality and fantasy which takes 'All poets are Jews' as its epigraph and as a theme. It's a journey in search of a 'Russian Jerusalem', a glittering pre-lapsarian world of poetic friendship, art and talk. 'There is an intensity to Russian friendship which is stronger than the passion of sexual love,' Feinstein tells us. Writing of the Silver Age poets she reveals she is 'infatuated with...their very being as much as their genius'.

In the company of Tsvetaeva's ghost – a 'sure-footed spectre' – Feinstein catapults herself through layers of history. Her language echoes Tsvetaeva's – 'the pathos of memory' plays on 'the revenge of memory'; there are black rivers, ice floes, bells; she travels through a 'shadowy world'. Along the way, we encounter Mandelstam, Pasternak, Babel, Brodsky and Akhmatova. Their stories interweave with Feinstein's quest for her own Russian Jewish roots. In one chapter, she visits her great-grandfather's *shtetl*. We are reminded that Pasternak's father visited Palestine in 1924, 'moved by some holy Jewish sepulchre'. When Mandelstam makes the fatal mistake of satirising Stalin, Feinstein imagines an 'ancient, tribal thought' in Pasternak's mind: '*a Jew should know better*'.

If Tsvetaeva spoke of 'people and cities that have been strongly inhabited by me', Feinstein attempts to inhabit Tsvetaeva's being ('I experience her desolate thoughts'). Her conceits of time-travelling ghosts and poets as Jews may be stretched at times, but the sheer verve of her storytelling fuses with her passion for the Russian poets she calls her 'extended family' to create a genuinely moving book that is ultimately about what home is.

Four days before she took her own life, Marina Tsvetaeva read 'Homesickness' aloud for Lidiya Chukovskaya. It's a poem that is as much about the pull of language as it is about place:

> And I won't be seduced by the thought of
> my native language, its milky call.
> How can it matter   in what tongue I
> Am misunderstood by whoever I meet...
>   – TRANSLATED BY ELAINE FEINSTEIN

'I belong to the Russian language. I am still a Russian poet,' Joseph Brodsky says in *The Russian Jerusalem*. Feinstein recalls a public clash with Brodsky about his belief in 'the necessity for rhyme' in translating Russian verse. Feinstein refutes this, insisting that 'more is lost than gained by insisting on strong full lines'. Nina Kossman, translator of Tsvetaeva's longer narrative poems in *Poem of the End*, agrees: 'Tsvetaeva's intensity, which in Russian perfectly agrees with her pattern of rhyme and rhythm, is bound to be lost whenever rhyme and metre become a translator's primary concern.' Other Tsvetaeva translators vehemently disagree. David McDuff believes 'it is necessary for any translator of Tsvetaeva's poetry to make at least some attempt to reproduce the formal and structural attributes of her poems... Without their forms, their harmonies and discords, Tsvetaeva's poems are simply – not there.' Robin Kemball echoes McDuff in his introduction to *Milestones*:

> ...for better or worse, the English versions given here reproduce, *mutatis mutandis*, the metres, rhythms, stanza forms, and rhyme pattern of the originals. It is no secret that this method does not commend itself to everyone... But this much we feel bound to say: as one reads and rereads the originals...it seems harder and harder to believe that any one of them could truly 'survive' translation in a different metre, let alone no metre at all. Even supposing (which is far from certain) that they emerged as good poems *in their own right* – what would be left of *Tsvetaeva* in the final reckoning?

It follows, then, that it is a brave poet or translator who takes on Tsvetaeva. It is worth noting that Tsvetaeva herself said 'what is writing poetry but translating from a native tongue to a foreign one? Orpheus bursts nationality.' She also stated that 'I do not fit into any form, not even the simplest form of my poems.'

For the most part, Belinda Cooke eschews a literal adherence to Tsvetaeva's edgy rhymes and jagged syntax; in their place is a plain language of everyday speech, a rendering that realises the sonorous can all too easily be ponderous in English. Thus Robin Kemball's 'There's nothing anyone's plundered' (from *Milestones*) becomes the simpler, more graceful 'no one has taken anything away'. Or compare the following:

> Inside my sonorous city cupolas shine,
> And the blind vagrant lauds his radiant Saviour...
> – And I hand you my city where church bells chime
> – Akhmatova – and my heart as an added favour!
>   – TRANSLATED BY ROBIN KEMBALL

> My city resounds. The domes shine.
> The blind beggar praises the bright Saviour.
> I give you my city of bells, Akhmatova,
> And my heart into the bargain.
>   – TRANSLATED BY BELINDA COOKE

Kemball's 'my / Tender sapling, wee / Featherlight-limbed tree' (from 'Poems of Moscow'), though, is a stroke of rhyming genius, and preferable to Cooke's more prosaic 'my little imponderable sapling'. An added challenge with Tsvetaeva is the very tone of her work ('I clang – blare – clap / I snarl, I shoot sparks'). Sound was central, and in her biography of Tsvetaeva, *Captive Lion*, Elaine Feinstein describes how 'she muttered and tried out words for their sound'. 'You must have an ear,' Tsvetaeva herself declared. Music was central to her work – as a young girl she composed her poems in a house filled with the sound of her mother's piano. In her essay 'Mother and music', Tsvetaeva recalls the profound impact of music on her psyche:

> The Chromatic scale, which I understood so much better than anything grammatical... the Chromatic is a whole inner structure of the heart and soul, and that structure is mine. Because the Chromatic, the most opposite thing there is to the grammatical, is the Romantic. And the Dramatic.
>
> It was the Chromatic that stayed there, lodged in my backbone.

Tsvetaeva's poems are defined for many by their urgent use of dashes, ellipsis and changes of word-order. These tropes had their origins in musical annotation ('I am making a row of marvellous violin clefs, one after the other, one after the other, fatter down below...But that was graphic, scribal, writer's ardour'). She was 'forced' to begin 'breaking up and dividing words into syllables...by the necessity of my rhythmic patterns.'

Poetry had to be *organic*, in much the same way that folk song might be. In her memoir, *Earthly Signs*, she says: 'for a poet to compose a folk song, the people must inhabit the poet. A folk song is not a rejection of self, but the organic coincidence, coalescence, consonance of a given "I" with the people's.' She disdained some poets for an 'un-Russianness... that coincided with the inorganic quality of their poetry.'

Tsvetaeva's ear, though, extends beyond music – her haunting account of the Russian Revolution, 'October on the Train', is charged with snippets of overheard chatter, gossip and argument as she travels across a Russia in chaos. Her prose and poetry are as informed by the demotic, the casual, the conversational, as they are by classic forms.

It is this sense of the demotic that feeds into one of Tsvetaeva's strengths – her ability to create a voice that is startling in its intimacy. For Belinda Cooke, 'a defiant hyperbole conceals an inner vulnerability'. In *Paths of the Beggar Woman*, Cooke probes beneath the dramatic forms of the Russian, seeking to find a voice for Tsvetaeva in English that can best reveal the *content* of the poems; she asks what is actually being *said*.

'There is nothing that is not symbolic,' believed Tsvetaeva. Poetry was the 'ark of the covenant', and her own poetry is suffused with the iconography of the Russian Orthodox Church. Her early collection *Milestones* is replete with references to the Virgin Mary, holy days, and the 'crimson cupolas' of Moscow's 'forty times forty' churches. Her poems of homage to Akhmatova and Blok ('Saint of God, beautiful, / you are the quiet light of my soul', Feinstein's translation) are almost religious in their adoration. At times her aphoristic lines echo the language of Biblical parable: 'the light will not go through the needle'; 'wretched are the strong and wealthy'; 'the thief gets in without the key'.

Whilst Cooke's versions owe much to Elaine Feinstein's, there are some startling differences, as in 'Insomnia':

> The sound of a footstep but no-one's there...
> (COOKE)

> Look at my steps – following – nobody...
> (FEINSTEIN)

> With the sound of your name comes a deep dream...
> (COOKE)

> About your name is: sleep...
> (FEINSTEIN)

Belinda Cooke's translations of Tsvetaeva into English, along with the other translations referenced here, are all, in their own way, essential. This is, quite simply, because Tsvetaeva herself is an essential poet. For the non-Russian reader, her original impulses have to be mapped out by a process of triangulation, comparing the alternative re-workings offered by different translators. Cooke has created an organic voice of her own for Tsvetaeva, marked by a sustained lyricism and rhythms that are natural and unstrained.

Writing of Tsvetaeva, Akhmatova once spoke of her 'trans-rational language'. Poetry and translation are both processes of movement from one mode of thought to another, of constantly looking at words and at the world in new ways. Or as Tsvetaeva put it:

> The piano was my first mirror and my first awareness of my face was through blackness, through its translation into blackness, as into a language dark, but comprehensible. That is how it was my whole life: to understand the simplest thing I had to plunge it into poetry, to see it *from there*.

Philip Coleman

EXTENDING THE PARAMETERS

Seán Lysaght, *The Mouth of a River* (Gallery Press, 2007), €11.95.
John McAuliffe, *Next Door* (Gallery Press, 2007), €11.95.

Reviewing a collection of essays on the work of Colm Tóibín recently,
John McAuliffe identified 'a weakness' in the discussion of the
'parameters of Irish fiction': 'like most Irish houses,' he suggested, they
'never seem to do anything but "extend"' ('Mastering Tóibín,' *The Irish
Times*, 28 June 2008). It's an interesting comment and, while it may
express impatience with the language of academic criticism, McAuliffe's
perhaps unwitting allusion to the Irish house of fiction as a space that has
had one too many 'extensions' in recent years is also intriguing. In 1908,
when Henry James advanced the notion of the 'house of fiction,' he
envisaged a structure 'which has in short not one window but a million.'
For the Master, moreover, 'there is fortunately no saying on what, for the
particular pair of eyes, the window may *not* open; "fortunately" by reason,
precisely, of this incalculability of range.' As he explained:

> The spreading field, the human scene, is the 'choice of subject'; the
> pierced aperture, either broad or balconied or slit-like and low-browed,
> is the 'literary form'; but they are, singly or together, as nothing without
> the posted presence of the watcher – without, in other words, the
> consciousness of the artist.

James contributed in a profound way to our sense of the novel and its
possibilities, and many writers after him have explored the range of writing 'either broad or balconied or slit-like and low-browed' forms. The best
prose writers of the last hundred years, from James Joyce to Joyce Carol
Oates, have sought to explore the possibilities available to them, and one
of the pleasures of reading them is in realising the extent to which they
'extend' the house of fiction.

If Colm Tóibín might be said to represent the very best of contemporary Irish fiction in terms of technique and thematic reach, however,
what about his peers in poetry? The question is too big to be broached
here, but the two books under review provide interesting examples, though
Seán Lysaght is the only one who can be considered a strict contemporary
of Tóibín's – Lysaght was born in 1957, Tóibín in 1955. Like Tóibín,
Lysaght likes to tell stories. At the centre of his latest collection is a
narrative sequence called 'The O———' which begins with an epigraph

from Lady Morgan/Sydney Owenson's epistolary novel *The Wild Irish Girl* (1806). The idiosyncratic title of Lysaght's poem refers in part to the strategic omission of letters in surnames and place names in Owenson's text: 'I leave Dublin to-morrow for M——— house. It is situated in the county of ———, on the north-west coast of Connaught, which I am told is the classic ground of Ireland.' Framed at the outset by this passage, and beginning with a piece that reconstructs a scene from the life of an engraver's assistant working on an illustrated edition of *The Wild Irish Girl*, Lysaght's poem seems then to offer an imaginative re-working of the world in which Owenson's text was made and a glimpse into the lives of those who made it. It soon becomes clear, however, that he is less concerned with examining early nineteenth-century constructions of 'the classic ground of Ireland' than he is with telling the story of the place named in the first part of the book, Tarsaghaunmore, which we are told is 'a wild, remote expanse of blanket bog with a number of spate rivers draining off the uplands' in the 'Notes and Acknowledgements' at the end of the book. These clarifications take away from the mysteriousness of 'The O———' as a presence in *The Mouth of a River*, and once Lysaght's speaker names 'every river he'd lived by' in the third section of the sequence – '*Owenmore, Owenglas, Owenwee, / Owenduff, Oweninny, Owengarve*' – it's hard to think of 'The O———' as something more than a river in Mayo, let alone a river that speaks with its own mouth.

One could say that 'The O———' is not a river poem at all but a poem that celebrates the fish who live in it. Sections III to VI describe salmon in various stages of their development, but then in section VII the reader encounters a character called Harry, and the poem turns in another direction to tell the story of Harry's desire to catch a salmon for no other reason, it seems, than to impress his wife Poppy. In these sections of the poem – Lysaght calls them 'Cantos' but the term doesn't really seem appropriate – the reader learns little details about Harry and his wife, but their story is nowhere as intriguing as the tale of Horatio M——— and Glorvina O'Melville in *The Wild Irish Girl*. Lysaght invites such comparisons, but chasing them is as futile as Harry's pursuit of a fish which, when all is said and done, he throws back into the river. Reading 'The O———' one is tempted to search for connections between Lysaght's text and Lady Morgan's, but the quest is ultimately pointless and it makes one wonder what Lysaght was trying to achieve, exactly, by referring to the earlier text at the start of the sequence. At times, indeed, it seems as if Lysaght is himself unsure about what he is doing in the poem, or how he should be doing it. He likes similes, as this random selection demonstrates: 'a peaty bank / like an old cow releasing the first water' (II); 'where running salmon crowded like memories' (III); 'when Slievemore / stood out like a canvas by Paul Henry' (XII); 'Have I given my vowels eyes /

like timber the craftsman finishes well?' (XXXII). In the last two examples here Lysaght seems to doubt his own ability to describe what he sees, and in section XVIII he gives up on simile altogether for a kind of abbreviated patter:

> Into the long track to Johnny's place.
> Park smartly. Get the waders out –
> all this bloody gear! Change from the shoes.
> Then the rod, connect the two sections,
> put the line through the rings, like a –
> no time for that now; forget scenery.
> Two flies, a shrimpy one at the end,
> with a bumble on the dropper (*Kingsmill Moore*).
> Test the knots. Get the bag and net.
> Car keys. Lock.

On the one hand these lines might be said to convey the excitement of Harry's quest, but who is speaking here? If it is Harry then he's surely right to forget the simile and get on with his fishing, but does the poet have an obligation to complete the figure? Moments such as this give the impression that Lysaght doesn't really know what he's doing in the poem. It's as if the poem is somehow greater than his ability to write it, which is another way of saying that it might have been more successful had he cast it in another form. Given its narrative impulse 'The O———' might have worked better as a short story, but as a poetic sequence it struggles to contain all that Lysaght has attempted to put into it – including the story of Harry and Poppy, Harry's friendship with an old farmer called Johnny, the locals' relationship with tourists and officials from the Heritage Service, the sense of place, the life of the river, fishing, Zen Buddhism, folklore, and the Irish language.

There is no reason, of course, why a poem *should* 'contain' its subject matter, and there are many examples of long poems or sequences that appear to resist all that their makers have put into them, from Ezra Pound's *Cantos* to Louis MacNeice's *Autumn Journal*. In section XXX of 'The O———' Lysaght writes: 'Bhí taibhsí i mo bhéal, ach ní raibh mé / ábalta iad a shamhlú i dteanga mo mháthar.' The lines' importance is signalled by their repetition at the end of the section, but they also point to a greater difficulty in Lysaght's collection to do with the articulacy and adequacy of poetic expression. Translation inevitably confronts such issues, and they are implicitly acknowledged in Lysaght's reworking of the medieval Irish poem *Buile Shuibhne* in *The Mouth of a River*, a story whose popularity in Seamus Heaney's version of it is also acknowledged in the book's notes. What makes Lysaght's version unique is his transformation of the disaffected cleric Sweeney into not one but many different kinds of birds – wigeon, smew, redwing, dabchick, cuckoo, eagle, hawk, tubenose, swallow, wagtail, and so on. As a cycle of poems in its own right Lysaght's 'Bird Sweeney' is more successful than 'The O———' and individual sections in it such as 'Leavings' and 'The Hawk in the Orchard' are altogether stronger than the clatter of lyrics with which the collection opens. The image of 'a eucharist of sandwiches' in 'Merlin at Tarsaghaunmore' together with the self-regarding posture of the speaker in 'A Discovery' ('how happily I walked / into the script of my own occasion') hastened this reader on to the book's middle section. *The Mouth of a River* is a very uneven collection overall, though, and while poems throughout the book echo each other in interesting ways the whole thing does not cohere in the way that the author seems to have intended. Lysaght was awarded the O'Shaughnessy Award for Poetry in 2007 and the judges praised the way that his 'work brings us not just to the natural world, but also to the environment of the imagination, the environment of language, the environment of literature and of the world's store of legend and tale.' There are snippets of folklore in Lysaght's work, and he does bring us to 'the natural world' of Tarsaghaunmore in his latest collection, but the book's mapping of 'the environment of language' or 'the environment of literature' is decidedly sketchy and could not be said to represent the kind of advance in writing suggested by the O'Shaughnessy judges. Compared with the environmental writing of Gary Snyder, for example, or the river poetry of Ted Hughes and, more recently, Alice Oswald, Lysaght's poems struggle to record the urgency of their occasions.

Lysaght is a poet of place, and so too is John McAuliffe, in a curious way. He is not an environmentalist poet like Lysaght, but he does have a very strong sense of his immediate environment and reading his poems a particular locale comes into view that is marked by images of domesticity, middle-class family life, and urban homeliness – 'The Quiet Life' as the title of one of the poems in *Next Door* puts it. The title of the collection simultaneously evokes ideas of neighbourliness and otherness that rest uneasily alongside each other in McAuliffe's work, and in this collection the poet's comfort zone – office, living-room, kitchen – often seems to be threatened by external forces and contexts. In 'Context' the reader encounters a private tutor trying to impress the importance of 'the *social*' upon a young female student struggling to come to terms with Shakespeare's *Measure for Measure*:

> '"There's vice that most
> I do abhor" – Relate

quotations to the title,
to the *social* as well
as to the personal'.

In his own work, McAuliffe often attempts to make the very same connection, relating personal observation to social context, but with mixed results. Some of the poems here offer neat descriptions of modern urban or suburban life, from the abandoned car in 'A Pyramid Scheme' to the 'middle-aged builders in the sunshine' who 'idle on the steps and bitch / about a friend of a friend's lottery win' in 'The Break'. But behind McAuliffe's poems of social observation – including these and others such as 'Damage', 'The Ice Carrier', and 'The Street' – there is a sense of discomfort in and unease with urban space that suggests the poet might be happier in Lysaght's Tarsaghaunmore than his adopted Manchester.

In 'Damage' the speaker quotes a 'nervous neighbour' who thanks God 'that nothing worse' happened when a tree 'fell / into the road / the other day'. The speaker seems to distance himself from her fears of 'what might have been...' (the ellipsis is in the original), but that fear of the unknown (inadequately expressed by the ellipsis) pervades McAuliffe's work also, despite the reassurances he offers himself in a number of the collection's poems. In 'The Hundred Towns', for example, the poet describes a family as they 'negotiate'

> ring road, tunnel and ferry
> but by noon GMT

> are nowhere, ie, an endless suburb
> stacked and balanced
> like washing-up.

> The day out seems set to fray
> into a relief map of noise,
> the kids crying *where*

> until you call a halt
> and we abandon the car
> and follow a sign pointing east

'I live for the wrong turns' the speaker announces at the start of McAuliffe's poem 'The Landing', but in this collection he comes across as the opposite of Baudelaire's *flâneur*, who delights in the experience of urban displacement. In 'The Hundred Towns' Czesław Miłosz's great poem 'Bypassing Rue Descartes' is quoted in an epigraph ('There is no capital of the world'), but McAuliffe's poem lacks the political and social urgency of the Polish poet's work, and in some respects the epigraph seems inappropriate for a piece that is more concerned with describing a suburban family's Sunday outing than it is with understanding 'the future of a hundred towns' mentioned almost too casually in one of the poem's step-down tercets. The formal arrangement of those tercets in itself doesn't seem to accomplish much in the scheme of the poem, and as they slide to a close in the final lines they announce the poet's inevitable return to the comfortable, the banal, that is worlds away from the existential strangeness experienced by Miłosz as he goes down to the Seine in 'Bypassing Rue Descartes.'

This is the problem with McAuliffe's poems: they often affect a certain worldliness that the poet himself or his speakers seem unwilling or unable to engage in without falling back on familiar signposts, maps, and all of the trappings that make the 'literary' possible, certainly, but also commonplace and dull. The book's closing poem ('The End of the World') describes the poet sitting in his new office, surrounded by 'desk, three chairs, some paper, / paper clips, two elastic bands, a hole puncher' *et cetera*. The speaker bemoans the lack of a printer ('an instruction manual for a printer. No printer.') but then realises – and this is the big moment in the poem – that 'nothing will happen / if I don't pick up when my number is called, / if I idle at the desk instead':

> looking at the tangle of strings
> that might operate the blinds,
> thinking about a pun, or a metaphor,
> and how,
>   as a matter of fact,
> it's not the end of the world.

It is not the end of the world that the poet doesn't have a printer, or if he doesn't pick up the phone when it rings, but the very idea that it could or should matter, somehow, speaks to a self-aggrandising notion of poetic selfhood that is more troubling than any of the images of social decay that appear throughout this collection. All the poet needs to do, McAuliffe suggests, is sit back and let things happen – 'thinking about a pun, or a metaphor' – but this works against an idea of poetic responsibility that Czesław Miłosz, for one, might advocate. In his Nobel Lecture in 1980 Miłosz said that 'whoever considers poetry as "to see and to describe" should be aware that he engages in a quarrel with modernity, fascinated as it is with innumerable theories of a specific poetic language.' McAuliffe's poems, it seems to me, are blissfully unaware of this quarrel, and for all of their immersion in the life of Irish and English towns and cities they ultimately yearn for a place that is beyond the noise – the 'buzz and weave' as he writes in 'The Hundred Towns' – of Miłosz's 'modernity.'

That said, there are moments of real tenderness in McAuliffe's collection, and he is at his best when he writes about family and home life, as in poems such as 'The First Person' (written in response to 'The Hospital' by Philip Larkin), 'By Accident', and 'Shouting Match', which provides four intimate portraits of parenthood. In the role of poet as *pater familias* McAuliffe is affecting, and sometimes amusing, but there is always the danger, as he puts it in 'The Yard', that 'the ball will land / on still-disputed land.' Although it is used here as an image out of childhood – the poem describes a brother and sister playing in their backyard – the piece also gives voice to a fear of that place beyond home that McAuliffe seems so uneasy about elsewhere in the collection. 'The yard can no more be split in two / than the house it backs onto / or is backed onto by' he writes in the same poem, summarising in a few lines his uneasiness with the world 'next door' – his neighbour, the other.

Lysaght and McAuliffe have now published over half a dozen books between them, and they have achieved considerable success as writers. Not only that, but readers of poetry in Ireland and elsewhere owe a huge debt of gratitude to McAuliffe, in particular, for the work he has done to promote poetry through the Poetry Now Festival in Dún Laoghaire, which he directed for a number of years, and for his work as an editor and reviewer in many publications, including this one. There are undoubtedly good things in *The Mouth of a River* and *Next Door*, and once again Peter Fallon and the Gallery Press have produced two beautiful books, complete with well-chosen and striking cover images. Reading them, however, one feels that these poets could be doing more to 'extend' the range of poetic expression. In language and form, in subject matter and theme, both Lysaght and McAuliffe are essentially doing the same things they have done in previous collections, but they are also attempting to make a kind of poetry that has been made better elsewhere, by better poets. Lysaght's latest book, *Venetian Epigrams*, translated from Goethe, begins with the following couplet: 'The little book shows, and thinks it funny. / The way you wasted time and money.' The lines mock the reader's misuse of years and euro, but they also poke fun at her or him for picking up the 'little book' in the first place. The question has nothing to do with whether a reader of these slim volumes gets value for money, but with the kind of aesthetic value they embody. Elsewhere in the *Epigrams* Lysaght writes (after Goethe):

Once they get to thirty I want every radical nailed to a cross.
As soon as a fool gets sense he's on a mission, and dangerous.

That's what's missing, finally, from the work of Lysaght and McAuliffe: radicalism, a sense of danger and, perhaps, a little bit of foolishness, without which 'the consciousness of the artist' (to use James's terms) is no different from that of any other man or woman on the street for whom the 'spreading field, the human scene' needs no further comment.

Notes on Contributors

Fergus Allen's most recent collection, *Gas Light & Coke*, was published by Dedalus Press in 2006. He lives near the Thames in moderately rural Berkshire.

Molly Bashaw was born in Malone, New York, USA, and grew up on a small farm. Following classical training as a musician at the Eastman School of Music, she moved to Stuttgart, Germany, where she has since worked as a professional trombonist and freelance translator. Her poetry has been published in a number of American journals, most recently in the *Beloit Poetry Journal*.

Nicholas Bradley is an eco-farm worker and gardener. He has worked in many Special Needs schools and has facilitated many poetry workshops. He received a Forward Poetry Prize nomination in 2004.

Paddy Bushe's poetry collections include *Poems With Amergin* (Beaver Row Press, 1989); *Teanga* (Coiscéim, 1990); *In Ainneoin na gCloch* (Coiscéim, 2001); *Hopkins on Skellig Michael* (Dedalus Press, 2001); *The Nitpicking of Cranes* (Dedalus, 2004); and *To Ring in Silence: New and Selected poems* (Dedalus Press, 2008).

Liam Carson is the director of the IMRAM Irish Language Literature Festival, and a publicist with publishing house Cois Life. His reviews, articles and essays have appeared in *Fortnight*, *The Irish Review*, *New Hibernia Review*, *Comhar* and the *Irish Examiner*.

Philip Coleman teaches in the School of English, Trinity College Dublin.

David Cooke gained first class honours in Modern Languages at Nottingham University in 1977, the same year his poetry earned him an E C Gregory Award. His first collection, *Brueghel's Dancers*, was published by Free Man's Press in 1984. He has been widely published in both Ireland and the UK. After a long absence he has started writing again, and has new work scheduled for publication in *Stand* and *Poetry Salzburg Review*.

John F Deane's latest poetry collection is *A Little Book of Hours* (Carcanet Press, 2008); his book of essays *From the Marrow-Bone* is published by Columba Press; and his most recent fiction is *The Heather Field and Other Stories* (Blackstaff Press, 2007).

Susie DeCoste is currently at work on a doctorate degree in Canadian literature at the University of Waterloo in Ontario, Canada. Her poetry has appeared in Canadian journals including *ARC*, *The Antigonish Review*, *The Fiddlehead* and *Grain* . This is the first of her poems to be published in Ireland.

Darrell Epp has had poems published in many magazines and journals, including *Saranac Review*, *POEM*, *Roanoke Review* and *Tears in the Fence*.

Carrie Etter has lived in England since 2001, and regularly visits her hometown of Normal, Illinois. She lectures in creative writing at Bath Spa University, and her first collection, *The Tethers*, will be published by Seren Books in the summer of 2009.

Jesse P Ferguson is the author of five poetry chapbooks, most recently *phoney phonetics* (No Press, 2007), and is widely published in print and online format. Editor of *The Fiddlehead*, a literary journal published in Fredericton, New Brunswick, his first full-length poetry collection is forthcoming in 2009 from Freehand Books.

Gina Ferrara works as an educator and lives in New Orleans near Bayou St John. Her chapbook, *The Size of Sparrows*, was published by Finishing Line Press. Her poems have appeared in numerous journals including *Poetry East*, *The Briar Cliff Review*, and *Callaloo*. Her latest collection of work, *Ethereal Avalanche*, will be published in early 2009 by Trembling Pillows Press.

Kit Fryatt is a lecturer in English at the Mater Dei Institute of Education, Dublin. She is involved in running Mater Dei's Irish Centre for Poetry Studies (**http://irishcentreforpoetrystudies.materdei.ie**), and co-edits its web journal, *POST*. She is the co-organiser of 'Wurm im Apfel', a series of poetry readings held at the Monster Truck Gallery in Dublin (**www.wurmimapfel.com**).

Miriam Gamble was born in 1980, and is a writer and critic, based in Belfast. She won an Eric Gregory Award in 2007, and her first pamphlet of poems, *This Man's Town*, was published by tall-lighthouse in 2007. Her poems have appeared in *Gallous*, *The Yellow Nib*, *Succour* and *The Scottish Review of Books*, and she has written reviews and features for *Fortnight*, *Tower Poetry* and the *New Statesman*.

Sam Gardiner was born in Northern Ireland and now lives on the Nunsthorpe Estate, Grimsby. His collection of poems *Southumbrian Tidings* reflect his experience of living in Grimsby and Cleethorpes over the last 40 years. He has published a number of works including two books *Protestant Windows* (2000) and *The Night Ships* (2007).

Enda Coyle-Greene lives in Co Dublin. Her first collection, *Snow Negatives*, won the Patrick Kavanagh Award in 2006 and was published in 2007 by Dedalus Press. She is currently studying for an MA in Creative Writing at Queen's University, Belfast.

Daniel Hardisty was born in Bradford in 1978. His poems have appeared in magazines and anthologies in the UK and in Ireland.

Tom Hubbard is a Scottish literary scholar and poet based at NUI, Maynooth. His most recent collection is *Peacocks and Squirrels* (Akros, 2007).

David Kennedy's recent publications include the poetry collection *The Devil's Bookshop* (Salt) and *Elegy* (Routledge New Critical Idiom). He is Senior Lecturer in English and Creative Writing at the University of Hull.

Thomas Kilroy is a playwright and novelist. His plays include *The Death and Resurrection of Mr Roche* (1968), *Talbot's Box* (1973), *Double Cross* (1986) and *The Shape of Metal* (2003). His novel *The Big Chapel* (Faber and Faber, 1971) was shortlisted for The Booker Prize.

James Liddy (1934–2008) was born in Kilkee, Co Clare. His first collection, *Esau, My Kingdom for a Drink*, was published by The Dolmen Press in 1962; his last, *On the Raft with Fr. Roseliep*, was published by Arlen House in 2006. He was a member of Aosdána, and lived and taught in Milwaukee, USA.

Richard Murphy's *Collected Poems* was published by Gallery Press in 2000. His awards include the Æ Memorial Award (1951); Fellow of the Royal Society of Literature (1969); and the American-Irish Foundation Award (1983). He is a member of Aosdána and lives in Sri Lanka.

Conor O'Callaghan teaches part-time both at Sheffield Hallam University and at Wake Forest University in North Carolina. His most recent collection is *Fiction* (Gallery Press, 2005).

Nessa O'Mahony lives in Dublin where she works as a journalist, editor and teacher. She has published two collections of poetry, *Bar Talk* (1999) and *Trapping a Ghost* (2005). A third collection, *The Side Road to Star*, is forthcoming from Bluechrome Publishing. She completed a PhD in Creative and Critical Writing in 2007.

Christina Park is a journalist and sub-editor living in Dublin. Her short story, *The Full Seven*, was published in the anthology *All Good Things Begin* (2006); her poetry has appeared in *The Big Issue Book of Home* (Hodder & Stoughton) and the Beehive Press poetry prizewinners' anthology, *Darkness and Light*.

Justin Quinn is an Irish poet and critic, born in Dublin in 1968. He received a doctorate from Trinity College, Dublin, and is a lecturer at Charles University in Prague.

Aidan Rooney grew up in Monaghan but now lives in Hingham, Massachusetts. He teaches at Thayer Academy and in the Teachers as Scholars program at Harvard University. His second collection of poems – *Tightrope* – appeared from Gallery Press in 2007.

Mark Roper has published five collections; the most recent is *Even So: New and Selected Poems* (Dedalus Press, 2008).

Knute Skinner lives in Co Clare. His collection *The Other Shoe* won the 2004-2005 Pavement Saw Chapbook Award. His most recent book, *Fifty Years: Poems 1957-2007* , from Salmon Poetry, contains new poems along with work taken from 13 previous books.

Gerard Smyth was born in Dublin where he still lives. His poetry has been published widely in literary journals in Ireland, Britain and the United States since the late 1960s. His most recent poetry collection, *The Mirror Tent,* was published in 2007 by Dedalus Press.

Howard Wright lectures in the history of fine and applied arts at the University of Ulster, Belfast. Recent poems have appeared in *The North, Cyphers* and *The Frogmore Papers*. His first full collection, *King of Country* is forthcoming from Blackstaff Press, Belfast.

Previous Editors of *Poetry Ireland Review*

John Jordan 1–8	Spring 1981–Autumn 1983
Thomas McCarthy 9–12	Winter 1983–Winter 1984
Conleth Ellis and Rita E Kelly 13	Spring 1985
Terence Brown 14–17	Autumn 1985–Autumn1986
Ciaran Cosgrove 18–19	Spring 1987
Dennis O'Driscoll 20–21	Autumn 1987–Spring 1988
John Ennis and Rory Brennan 22–23	Summer 1988
John Ennis 24–25	Winter 1988–Spring 1989
Micheal O'Siadhail 26–29	Summer 1989–Summer1990
Máire Mhac an tSaoi 30–33	Autumn 1990–Winter 1991
Peter Denman 34–37	Spring 1992–Winter 1992
Pat Boran 38	Summer 1993
Seán Ó Cearnaigh 39	Autumn 1993
Pat Boran 40–42	Winter 1993–Summer 1994
Chris Agee 43–44	Autumn/Winter 1994
Moya Cannon 45–48	Spring 1995–Winter 1995
Liam Ó Muirthile 49	Spring 1996
Michael Longley 50	Summer 1996
Liam Ó Muirthile 51–52	Autumn 1996–Spring 1997
Frank Ormsby 53–56	Summer 1997–Spring 1998
Catherine Phil MacCarthy 57–60	Summer 1998–Spring 1999
Mark Roper 61–64	Summer 1999– Spring 2000
Biddy Jenkinson 65–68	Summer 2000–Spring 2001
Maurice Harmon 69–72	Summer 2001–Spring 2002
Michael Smith 73–75	Summer 2002–Winter 2002/3
Eva Bourke 76	Spring/Summer 2003
Peter Sirr 77–91	Autumn 2003 / October 2007
Eiléan Ní Chuilleanáin 92–95	December 2007 / October 2008

Creativity Test

Poetry Ireland Review

Subscription Rates

Ireland/Britain
One Year   - €40
Two Years - €75

Overseas
One Year   - €50
Two Years - €95

Poetry Ireland News
One Year   - €10
Two Years - €18

Subscribe online on poetryireland.ie/publications

Poetry Ireland
2 Proud's Lane, *off* St. Stephen's Green, Dublin 2
t 01 4789974 **f** 01 4780205 **e** info@poetryireland.ie